Coach 'Em Up!
Skip Hall

Praise for *Coach 'Em Up*

Skip has been a phenomenal coach with an infectious personality since the beginning of our acquaintance in the 1960s. He also proved to be a sensational recruiter over the many years that I have known him. Everyone will learn something from his story.

—Mike Lude, former Athletic Director University of Washington

The lessons I learned from Skip are timeless and will continue to propel me through life. I now know that I will always have the strength and ability to come out the other end.

—Lori Murphy, Phoenix Businesswoman

Skip Hall is a great storyteller and has a lifetime of wisdom to share. He has successfully applied his life-values and principles on three fronts: coaching, business, and ministry. This book beautifully draws Skip's story and captures his essence. The result is extremely satisfying and the truths and teachings go far beyond just being an enjoyable story.

—Jon Strain, You Gotta Ask, Inc.

One of the great joys of my life was to play Linebacker for the University of Washington Huskies and to be coached by Skip Hall. Not only did Coach Hall inspire, challenge, and motivate us on the field, he mentored and taught us how to be men of character off the field. He instilled greatness in us for life. I am forever grateful for his tremendous impact on my life.

—Mike Rohrbach, 1977 UW Husky Co-Captain, 1978 UW Husky Rose Bowl Captain, Run2Win founder and CEO

Skip Hall has lived a life rich in experience, status, and recognition. These are all great, but they don't overly impress me because of their fleeting nature. What does impress me is a person of character. He has always leaned into turning problems into opportunities, inspiring people to become the best version of themselves, and serving a higher purpose in life. I am very grateful for this book, both because of the wonderful stories of a life well lived and to point all of us to living for something beyond ourselves.

—Ron Price, CEO Price Associates, author of *The Complete Leader: Everything You Need to Become a High-Performing Leader* and *Growing Influence*

Coach Hall was the kind of coach that cared about the heart behind the jersey. He was focused on improving skill and winning games, but not at the expense of the players' heart and character.

—Ken Lewis, Idaho FCA Director

Coach Hall is a man of great faith, great character, and a great competitive drive. As the head coach, he surrounded our program with players and coaches that I wanted to play for and compete with. In doing that, he brought out the best in me.

—Erik Helgeson, Boise State football Hall of Fame inductee and most honored football player in Boise State history

Coach Skip Hall taught me many things, but the biggest thing that he ever drilled into me was that the game is not the most important thing. He taught me with his words and example that it's not the score that matters, but who you come home to after the game, win or lose. He is truly a great man with an even better perspective.

—Jeff "Monty" Montgomery, former Mizzou football player and Grad Assistant Coach

I found out soon after meeting Coach Hall that he was a talented coach with high integrity. He showed me in many ways that he cared about me and the other players. That made the biggest difference in my life at the time. Caring about the players is what I carried into my own coaching career, and I am truly grateful.

—Travis McDonald, former professional football player and Lead Therapeutic Intervention Coach, Salem, Oregon

A coach is someone who gets excited about helping others be successful by coming alongside and sharing their experience and expertise in a relevant manner so that those people can succeed. Skip Hall is the perfect example of this not only on the field, but also in churches and offices.

—Larry Glabe, Staff Representative, The Navigators

I am impressed with his magnetism and how he approached people and made them feel. He didn't only encourage players on the football field, but he "coached up" everyone he recruited to be their most successful selves.

—Ron Sanders, Aflac Director of Sales for U.S. Operations

COACH 'EM UP
The Skip Hall Story

How the Power of Influence
and Encouragement Changes Lives

Foreword by Coach Nick Saban
Seven-Time National Champion

Coach Skip Hall
Three-Time Hall of Fame Recipient, Seven-Time College Bowl Champion
with Heather Goetter

Coach 'Em Up: The Skip Hall Story
How the Power of Influence and Encouragement Changes Lives
By Skip Hall © 2021

Book Production by Aloha Publishing
Co-Author: Heather Goetter
Cover and Interior Design by: Fusion Creative Works, FusionCW.com
Picture Credit: James Macari, Katelyn Kristine Photography, Steve Jones, Pete Grady, and the Hall Family Collection

For more information, visit CoachEmUpBook.com

To purchase this book at discounted prices, go to AlohaPublishing.com or email alohapublishing@gmail.com.

Print ISBN: 978-1-61206-237-2
eBook ISBN: 978-1-61206-239-6

Published by

AlohaPublishing.com

Printed in the United States of America

To Virginia, Suzie, and Chris & Jennifer because we have always been a team.

To our grandchildren and great-granddaughter, Cassidy & Vince, Jadyn & Gibson, Tyler, Austin, and Selah, I love how our team keeps getting bigger and better.

To my mentors for shaping me into who I am today, especially Coach Charlie Basch, Coach Jake Christiansen, Coach Don James, Chuck Snyder, and Chuck Swindoll.

And to my Lord and Savior Jesus Christ.

◄ CONTENTS ►

"A coach will impact more people in one year than the average person will in an entire lifetime."

—Billy Graham

Foreword

Written by Nick Saban

Seven-time NCAA Football National Champion

Skip Hall and I go way back . . . in fact, our friendship dates to 1970 when "The James Gang" first set foot on the campus of Kent State University. I was a defensive back for the Golden Flashes and Skip was a young up-and-coming coach on staff. The legendary Don James was the head football coach . . . one of, if not *THE* best collegiate coaches who ever was, both personally and professionally. It didn't take long for Skip, as a coach, and me, as a player, to learn a valuable lifelong lesson: mentors make a difference. The Kent State anti-war protests and tragic fatalities in May of 1970 were fresh in the minds and hearts of America; needless to say, Skip had to overcome adversity right from the start of his college coaching career.

When my playing days came to an end, my wife, Terry, was still working toward her degree so, instead of going back to West Virginia to take over operations of the family business, I heeded the advice of Coach James and stayed on as a defensive graduate assistant. It was then that my career path changed forever, as I found out how much I loved coaching. A year later, I became a bona fide KSU coach and Skip and I ended up coaching together for two years . . . he on the offensive side of the ball, and me on defense. We made a good team.

Skip and I adopted the Don James coaching philosophy, believing that, in addition to coaching our team on the field, it was equally important to develop our players off the field. We had a solid life skills program that was readily embraced by our players, encouraging them to be the best version of themselves, and teaching them how to build their brand. Skip and I stressed the importance of cultivating and securing strong, meaningful, lasting relationships and serving others in the communities where our players resided. Many found gainful employment or went on to play professional football. This was a bit of an anomaly for a football program in the 1970s!

When the media asks me about the success of 2020 Alabama Heisman Trophy winner DeVonta Smith, I simply reply, "His performance speaks for itself." I would say the same about Skip. His leadership inspires and influences all who are lucky enough to know him. He always went above and beyond to encourage his players and fellow coaches. Take the lessons learned from this book and apply them to your own life; share them with your family and friends . . . and with your teams.

"We all benefit when we are 'coached up'
to reach our full potential."

–Nick Saban

The Making of *Coach 'Em Up*

A note from co-author Heather Goetter

It has been an honor and a privilege to assist Coach Skip Hall in writing this book. When he came to us at Aloha Publishing in the fall of 2020 and expressed his desire to write his story and share with others about all the ways God has blessed him throughout his life, we were excited. Maryanna Young, who heads the team at Aloha Publishing, has known Skip for more than 20 years. She first met him while he was the head coach at Boise State. Over the years they had talked about the need and desire for Skip to share his story and she was very ready to help him with the daunting task.

Maryanna brought me in to do the actual writing of his story. The journey has been filled with discovery, encouragement, laughter, hard work, and friendship. We interviewed Skip almost weekly for six months and did more than 40 interviews with friends, family, players, fellow coaches, and mentors. We sorted through photo after photo of his life, his friends, and his career. He presented his story with humility, humor, loyalty, and a few tears. Through this process, we have seen his passion for football, recruiting, individuals from all walks of life, student athletes, other coaches, friends, and family. We have also seen Skip's focus on God above all. Many of the stories you will read have never been told before.

Throughout the production of this book, three things became crystal clear to me:

1. Skip is a connector. He loves to help people by connecting them to other people, opportunities, and those who can help them succeed.

2. Skip is a recruiter for all the right reasons. He loves to offer people opportunities that will benefit them. He gets excited about assisting others in their future careers and friendships, and about accelerating their potential.

3. Skip loves God. He wants God to direct his life and wants to share that love with others. He reflects his relationship with Jesus by how he lives his life.

We have seen these three things, not only from Skip's words but from the words of his family, friends, players, and mentors. Each and every person we interviewed has a deep love and admiration for Skip. Before writing the book, our team had huge respect for Coach Hall. Our respect grew even more when we talked to some of the most important people in his life, including his family, friends, players, and mentors.

I personally am so grateful we were given the opportunity to share Coach Skip Hall's life story and his coaching lessons with you. Your coaching style and interactions with your family members, your friends, your fellow coaches, your business associates, and how you grow your relationship with God will be forever changed.

◄ INTRODUCTION ►

Coach 'Em Up

I looked up from my new desk in my new office at the University of Missouri, surprised at the knock. Though I had only been there a few weeks, not many people knocked on my door. They usually just walked in when they needed me. I hollered a "Come in!" and leaned back in my chair to see who was about to walk through my door.

It was 1993 and I had been a coach for more than 25 years. Throughout those years, many players, coaches, assistants, and athletic administrators had walked through my door. I knew that each person who came into my life was there for a reason.

In walked a gentleman. He was dressed in casual everyday clothes and looked to be in his early 30s. He looked vaguely familiar, but I couldn't be sure if I had known him before or not.

I greeted him with a handshake, and he introduced himself like this:

"Coach Hall, you won't remember me, but 10 years ago, I was a walk-on player and you were an assistant football coach at the University of Washington. During one of our first practices, I was really messing up; fumbling, stumbling, and falling. One of the coaches was yelling at me. He was insulting me, cursing at me, and putting me down in front of the entire team. He was so loud and angry that it caught your attention. You walked over and got in between the coach and me. As I stood there, I expected you to correct me, but instead you looked at the young coach and said five words I will never forget, 'Coach 'em up, not down.'"

He went on to tell me that those five words had made a huge impact on his life. They changed the way he treated others. He told me the most-requested sermon he ever gave was called "Coach 'Em Up, Not Down."

This young man was a pastor in a small town about an hour away, and as soon as he had heard I was coaching at the University, he hopped in his car and drove down to talk to me. He wanted to tell me this story and thank me for the impact it had on his life.

I thanked him for the encouragement, then we talked a bit more and he headed home.

After he left, I leaned back in my chair and thought about the first time I had heard those same words spoken to me.

It was our second year at the University of Washington. All of the coaches were struggling. People weren't happy. We weren't winning enough. A lot of the players hadn't bought into the football program and most were also dealing with personal problems.

Every morning we would have a staff meeting and every position coach would have to go over his players and give a report on how and what they were doing. During one of the meetings, I was really frustrated. When it was my turn to give a report to our head coach, Don James, I complained, saying, "You know, I've got players who are sick, players who are hurt. I've got players with girlfriend problems, academic problems, and family problems." I went on and on and on. After I had finally finished my rant, Coach James looked at me and simply said three words.

"Coach 'em up."

Those three words changed my whole coaching perspective. I stopped worrying about all the problems and focused on coaching up the men I had. I stopped trying to solve their problems and started focusing on building up the men's characters.

When I changed my focus, everything changed. I made people my top priority. I focused on each person, the individual, and not their problems. I began to coach them on how to react to difficult situations, how to become proactive in their personal lives, and how to make the best choices to become men of integrity. When I did that, not only did these men I was coaching change, but I changed too. It increased my capacity to care. I started seeing them for who they were: talented men struggling in a challenging world. I truly started caring about them.

And when I cared about them, two character qualities grew within me: strength and warmth.

I remember having an impactful encounter with a college coaching giant that drove home to me the quality of warmth. I was a graduate assistant at the University of Colorado Boulder where I was getting my master's degree. That first year I was there, we played and beat Alabama in the Liberty Bowl in Memphis. After the bowl game in those days, they had a banquet. During the banquet, I was heading to the restroom when out of the restroom, coming right at me, was none other than Coach Bear Bryant. I was awestruck.

I mustered up enough courage to say, "Coach Bryant, I just want to thank you for all you've done for the profession." He took my hand in his big old paw, looked me in the eye after glancing at my name tag and said, "Skipper, how have you been?" like we'd known each other for years, even though he had never seen me before that day. It hit me then that warmth can make a huge impact on a person and it is one of the top two attributes of a leader.

In football, coaches often think of strength in leadership. When coaches are strong, they have resolve, they know how to get things done, they don't get pushed around. Strength will get their team on the field, lead them to victories, and give them authority—but warmth is not usually at the top of coach character qualities. Warmth shows you care about the person. Warmth encourages relationships and builds others up. The thing is, when your men know you care about them, they work hard and try to do their best. They give you their best.

One of my best coaches, Coach Charlie, showed both strength and warmth to me for seven years of my life as a teenager and young man. He portrayed God's heart and character to me more than any other man during those years. I truly wanted to do and be better for him.

The challenge of "coach 'em up" was given to me as a young coach, and throughout my career I gave it to others. Now I'm giving it to you.

Coach 'em up, not down.

◄ 1 ►

Four States, Two Fathers

My birth name was Merlin Dale Erickson, but my mom and brother always called me Merle. I grew up with everyone calling me this name. The story of how I got the name "Skip" comes later.

I was born in Minneapolis, Minnesota, on February 18, 1944, to Marcella "Marcy" Erickson and Morden Erickson, her first husband and my father. I am 75 percent Norwegian and 25 percent Swedish, so I like to say that I am Scandihoovian.

We lived in Minneapolis for the first three years of my life and my mom took care of me while my dad sold insurance. Around my third birthday, my dad was offered a job opportunity in San Francisco, California, where his brother lived, so we packed everything up and moved across the country.

My brother, Duane, was born the year after we moved to San Francisco, in 1948. He was four years younger than me. I was young and carefree for three years in California, until Duane was about two years old. I had been mostly unaware of the arguing and drinking in the house. My mom did a really good job of protecting my brother and me from my dad's drunkenness, but he'd gotten progressively more violent, and she'd soon had enough. She filed divorce papers and moved us to Seattle, Washington, where my Uncle

Everett, my mother's brother, was the manager of the naval housing project. She and Uncle Everett had always been close, and he had offered to help her with housing and us boys. I was six years old.

Me, my brother Duane, and my mom in 1949

My mother, Duane, and I moved into the naval housing project. We had a small house close to Uncle Everett's office and the elementary school I attended. Our neighborhood was safe and lots of kids would run around, giving us companions to play with. My mom got a job at the Veterans of Foreign Wars (VFW) office and was gone during the day. We lived close enough to Uncle Everett's office that we could reach him if we needed anything. We spent much of our time on the playground of the elementary school, but we'd also ride our bikes around, or do other fun things like slide on cardboard down the hill behind our little housing unit.

When I was little, Uncle Everett was kind of the man of the house—we didn't live with him, but still we saw him almost every day. He was single so we were his family. Duane and I would sometimes go to his house near the government locks and watch the boats come and go. He had tons of flowers growing in the front and back yards. We would have dinner with him regularly. He loved to cook and was really good at it. He always made the holiday meals.

The Naval Housing Project where we lived in Seattle, Washington

Uncle Everett Edenloff was a unique person. He was a talented singer and sang in groups and churches, with the choir and solo. Much later in life, he sang at my daughter's wedding and my mother's funeral. He also loved birds—canaries specifically, maybe because they sing. I remember one day when I was still little, my brother and I were bird-sitting Uncle Everett's bird, and we let it out of the cage. Well, that little bird got so excited he dropped over dead from a heart attack.

We sometimes called my uncle by his initials, "EPE," and he was very funny and warm because he was always goofing around with us. We even sometimes called him Uncle Everett the Goof. He was fun but made sure we behaved and was there for us whenever our mother was working.

Seattle was the beginning of my sports-life—even as a young kid. I attended View Ridge Elementary School and during that time, sports became a big deal to me. Throughout the year, I was always playing some kind of sport, and I loved it. I thrived playing as many sports as possible.

One of the happiest and saddest memories I have of my life in Seattle is about Captain, our German shepherd. Both my brother and I loved Captain and would play with him whenever we weren't at school or with Uncle Everett. Unfortunately, we had to give him away a couple years later because we didn't have enough room for him in our little place. We found a good home in the country for him, but I still think about Captain. He began in me a great love for dogs that I still have to this day.

I have always loved dogs

While we lived in Seattle, we occasionally went to the local Lutheran church, but we were what I now like to call "two-timers," the Christmas and Easter folks. I didn't think much about God or the Bible. But I did know right from wrong and telling the truth from lying, because I was taught that. Because we were two-timers, I didn't grow up having a personal relationship with the Lord. However, that changed later and I am eternally grateful.

My father visited us one time when we were living in Seattle. He and I walked into the woods near our house and he asked me questions as we walked. But my mother had told me to only be polite and not to get too close to him, because he was going to take off again.

"He's gonna take off and do what he does," she'd said. I answered his questions politely but didn't do more than that, knowing I wouldn't see him very much. I definitely didn't get my hopes up that he would be around more.

Though we saw my Uncle Everett almost every day, we didn't see much of the rest of my mom's family in Minnesota. One time my mom created a recording of me singing "Zippity-Doo-Dah" for my grandma on a 45 record. We sent it to her in the mail. I still remember the words to this day. I know my mom did talk to her mom, dad, and other brothers occasionally. She kept them informed about how we were doing and what we were up to and sent them pictures of us in the mail.

While in Seattle, my mother met a man named William Clinton Hall at the VFW. He was a veteran of WWII and would hang out at the VFW. They got acquainted and started dating. I first met Clint when he came to the house to pick up my mom for a date. He was nice, good looking with dark hair, and fairly tall—6'1" or 6'2". He took the time to talk to me and ask me questions before he and Mom left for their date. After that, I started to see him more frequently as he and mom got more serious. I could tell that my mom was happier and because of that, I decided he was a good guy.

My mom and Clint Hall got engaged about a year later. They had a small wedding ceremony in the little Lutheran church near our house, after which we packed up and moved to Moscow, Idaho, where Clint lived and worked.

My few years in Seattle were happy ones. We had a stable, quiet home with lots of friends in the neighborhood and local school. I had started to wear the man-of-the-family hat, watching my little brother, helping Mom with the manly chores, and trying to do some of the things around the house she couldn't because she worked full time. To leave all that and move into someone's house, in another state, and start another school was scary. And I would miss Uncle Everett. Thankfully, I knew Mom would be there for me no matter what and I was glad she had found someone to make her happy and help financially.

Life in Moscow

I started fourth grade in Moscow, Idaho. The school was small and most of the kids were friendly. It was Duane's first time in school, and he really liked the kindergarten and made friends quickly. I had started playing Little League baseball in Seattle and was happy to keep playing in my new state and new school.

My new stepdad had a business tiling fields for farmers. To tile fields, he dug ditches in fields and laid clay drainage pipes to carry off unwanted water so the crops could get enough oxygen to their roots. He would occasionally take me with him to work when I was little, but mostly he left early and came home late, tired and dirty.

For a few years, we were a normal family with a dad, of sorts. My stepdad would take us camping and fishing as well as do other regular family stuff. He would sometimes get frustrated with my brother and me.

My stepfather would say mean things off the cuff like, "You'll never amount to anything."

But mostly he was a good guy—except when he drank. He and my mom would get into arguments about his drinking. She never yelled at us, but she'd yell at him. It was unfortunate that the two guys she married both had a problem with drinking. As I got a little older, I started to wonder if the same thing would happen that happened with my real father.

Maybe I should have been a cowboy

Thankfully, Duane was a happy-go-lucky, seemingly oblivious boy when he was elementary age. He loved having fun and being funny. He quickly became the class clown in school and, though he never got in serious trouble, he loved goofing around. Many of his teachers were exasperated by his antics. Duane had a soft side too and it showed in his love for animals. We had both a dog and a rabbit in Moscow. We used to have the rabbit in a cage outside the house. The rabbit had a little patch of brown fur right by his nose, so we named him Dirty Nose. Duane loved both the dog and the rabbit and always asked for more pets, though my mom put her foot down about that. He loved to do taxidermy and learn about all kinds of animals.

The four-year age difference felt like a big gap between Duane and me, though we did play together quite a lot. We both loved to play on the local playground. We spent hours there playing with friends. There were times when we got along really well and times when we would fight. One time when I was mad at Duane, I chased him down the street. I ended up tripping and falling on my face and knocked out half of my front tooth.

As I got older, I started acting more like a teenager. I didn't want my little brother hanging out with me when I was with my friends, so I made him walk four steps behind me. He was annoyed but couldn't do much about it. He would just watch my friends and I interact with our teenage antics. As I got older, I would think back about how I treated him and feel bad. After growing out of that stage, I made sure I never treated anyone like that again.

Junior High, Sports, and a New Name

My first official job was as a pinsetter at the University of Idaho bowling alley when I was 14. Those were the days before they automated the process to load the setting machines. It was all done by hand and the bowling alley hired kids like me to work in the evening and on weekends. We'd have to jump into the pit to pick the pins up and then load them in the machine. We also had to send the ball back. It was good to work hard and make money and I worked as much as possible.

Later during my junior high school years, I worked with my stepfather at his business when I wasn't playing sports. He had a really good work ethic and taught me how to work in the fields laying tile and how to run the backhoe. However, sports were always front and center.

I played every sport I could, every chance I had. I couldn't get enough.

I played on a Little League baseball team, Wholesome Bakery, back when the teams were named after the sponsor. I played third base and I pitched. I ended up winning a little all-star gold pendant, which I gave to my first official girlfriend, Gayle, when I was 14.

For years, I played basketball in the park for fun. I'd play with friends such as Lonne Pedersen and Keith Hurdstrom, who I remained friends with throughout our lives. I'd shoot baskets if nobody was available to play pickup in the neighborhood. In eighth grade, I started to play organized basketball as well.

In junior high, I listened to the University of Idaho Vandal football games on the radio and went to the basketball games. I was the Vandal batboy as well. The coaches saw me hanging around frequently because we lived close to the ballpark. I would be there watching or shagging balls, and they asked me to be their batboy.

While we lived in Moscow, Idaho, my stepfather adopted my brother and me. This is where the name Hall came from, through that adoption. Though it was a little strange to have a different last name, it was nice to have my mom's last name again. I was now officially Merle Dale Hall.

Sadly enough, that marriage ended in divorce four years later, in the middle of my ninth-grade year. Like with my real dad, my mom decided she couldn't handle the drinking and fights and didn't want us to bear the brunt of it either. I was worried about my mom. I had seen her have to work so hard in Seattle. How was she going to do that all over again? I was also sad that we would probably have to move. I had just started playing football and was a quarterback, which I absolutely loved.

Once again I was fatherless. I had only experienced having a father for a few short years of my life, but I knew something was missing. My mom was amazing, working and taking care of us, but I longed for a male role model who could give me advice as I was turning into a man. Little did I know that the next chapter of my life would bring me that exact person.

◄ 2 ►

High School, Sports, and Lifelong Connections

Immediately after the divorce in 1959, Uncle Leroy, one of my uncles from Minnesota, flew out and helped us pack up our stuff in the new 1957 Chevy my stepdad had just bought for my mom. We drove to Osakis, Minnesota, where my mother's dad lived, to start a new life. My grandmother had died at age 54, but my grandfather, Vic Edenloff Sr., lived there with Uncle Leroy. They had a big house and we moved in with them and enrolled in the local schools there—Duane in elementary and I as a freshman in high school. We started halfway through the school year in 1959.

Soon after we arrived in Minnesota, my mother got a job as the traffic manager at the TV station (Channel 7) in Alexandria, Minnesota, which was about a 10-mile commute from my grandpa's house.

On my very first day at the new school in Osakis, the basketball coach pulled me out of class and took me down to the gym because he heard I was an athlete. We worked one-on-one with each other. He immediately put me on the team—the B team *and* the varsity.

One of my first games in freshman basketball was against the bigger high school in Alexandria, Jefferson Senior High School. We beat them. It was kind of a David-versus-Goliath game. Alexandria was a much larger high school with a pretty serious sports program.

They weren't used to getting beaten—especially by a small-town, no-name high school, but we were good. We had a pretty good combination; there were two big guys on the inside, and I was on the outside—the outside shooter, the playmaker, so to speak. I fed the inside guys and they would score. We were quite a team. I thought if I had stayed and if we had developed a game strategy with those guys, we would have had a great run at the state championship.

After that one game, when the Alexandria coaches heard that my mother worked in Alexandria, the wheels started spinning and they realized it would be better if we moved there. They were able to convince my mother to move and even found us a place to rent that we could afford. We moved to Alexandria during the summer, after the school year was out. Our apartment was a block away from the brand-new high school. My sophomore year was the first sophomore class in the new building.

I again played every sport I could, starting with football, basketball, and baseball.

My high school football team (I'm number 14)

The town, school, and coaches took football much more seriously in Alexandria. All the players got a little playbook, and we'd watch 16-millimeter film of the past games. If the coaches knew something about the other team, they would share it with us and talk us through the game plan. I started as a quarterback—right from the beginning.

All my coaches seemed to see something in me and would put me in a position of leadership. I thrived in leadership roles. It seemed like I knew what needed to get done and I had the ability to motivate others to work toward that goal. And I was no slacker. I would be right in there with my teammates, working as hard or harder.

The coaches I had were the stable men in my life. They played the job of dad and mentor to me. In addition to coaching me on the football field, they also asked and gave advice about my social and home life.

These men showed me, more than told me, how to act with integrity, honesty, and self-confidence.

Coach Charlie Enters the Picture

The summer of my sophomore year, one of the most influential coaches in my life entered the picture. His name was Coach Charlie Basch. He coached the summer American Legion baseball team and also played on the town team I joined that summer. We played together against other towns and cities around us and it was mostly older guys on the teams.

When I first met Coach Charlie, he welcomed me with open arms. He had heard about me playing for Osakis High School and knew I was moving to Alexandria. One morning I went down to the ballpark because I knew they were having practice. I went out and introduced myself and asked him what I could do to be a part of what they were doing. He invited me to join.

Coach Charlie Basch wrote me an encouraging
message on my senior yearbook

We immediately connected and worked together on those two summer teams. He was a very winsome, encouraging, open person. He encouraged me when I messed up, inspiring me to try harder and do better. He never yelled at the team or put them down like some other coaches. Charlie became a solid mentor in my life right from the beginning, showing me and telling me how to be a man of integrity. He was also a joyful man and fun to be around.

Charlie was the football and baseball coach for the Alexandria high school, Jefferson Senior High. He ended up coaching my sports teams for three straight years in those sports. He eventually coached me in college as well.

My sophomore year of high school was great. Not only was I playing sports I loved with a coach I loved, but I also started to get to know my peers and made lifelong friendships and connections.

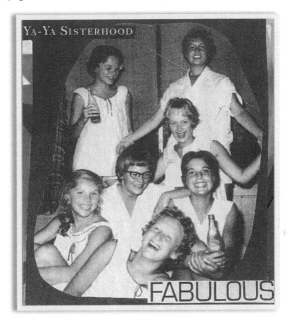

Girl's of '62

Girl's of '62 when they recreated their original photo decades later

That first year, I dated a cute, blonde, peppy little cheerleader named Marcy Osterberg. She was a part of a group of girls from our high school that later became known as the "Girls of '62." After high school, they would get together every year or so for a few days to hang out. This has been going on for more than 50 years now.

In football that year, I played as a backup quarterback. In basketball, I was a backup guard, and in baseball, I started on the varsity team mainly playing third base and occasionally pitching.

Not having a father in my life like all my friends was hard but felt normal to me at that point. Unfortunately, my lack of a father was drilled home one day—the last time I ever saw my real father.

He unexpectedly came to watch me play a basketball game in my sophomore year of high school. At the time I was with my second girlfriend, Marcy. Her dad co-owned Osterberg Café, so after the games we'd go there to have a hamburger and shake. After one particular game, my real dad walked into Osterberg Café, walked up to our booth, and asked, "Are you Merle?"

Though I knew who he was, I said no.

My response was kind of shocking as I think back about it now, but I responded that way because of my mother's influence. She didn't want us, my brother or me, dealing with him.

By my junior year, I realized I couldn't play sports my whole life. Coach Charlie had become a father figure to me. I determined that if I couldn't play sports, I wanted to be a coach like Charlie. He taught me how to encourage people by building them up and not putting them down. He was understanding and had a great sense of humor. I knew that I wanted to be like him when I grew up. I used to think, "If I can make $8,000 a year and be like Coach Charlie, boy, that would be great!"

In my junior year, I became the starting quarterback in football, starting guard in basketball, and starting third baseman in baseball. It was a good year not just in sports but also with my teammates. David

Erickson was a teammate in baseball and basketball. He was a tremendous encourager and we have stayed friends for almost 60 years.

I had a great basketball team at Jefferson Senior High School

At the end of my sophomore year, Marcy and I had stopped dating, but we remain friends to this day. I began dating a girl named Joan, who was another cute blonde cheerleader. She also became part of the Girls of '62. We dated through our entire junior year but broke up at the end of the year and are still good friends as well.

Coach Charlie continued to be a huge influence and father figure to me that year. He was a great coach and mentor. Many people would say, "Man, that guy is really something." I thought the same thing. *That's who I want to be like*, I decided. Charlie was always laughing and smiling. He used to tease me about my girlfriends. He was able to relate to the students well because he was only 17 years older.

During my entire high school sports career, my mom was a huge support. She would come to as many basketball and baseball games as her schedule allowed. She'd be the loudest one there, cheering me and my teammates on. Funnily enough, she never wanted to come to my football games. She always worried about me getting hurt and decided it was better to worry from home than to watch and wait. So she mostly listened to the games on the radio at home.

Playing basketball in high school

During the last couple of years of high school, I was always looking for work that would give me spending money. Three or four guys from my class got connected to a job working for the local newspaper two to three nights a week. We sorted the sections and put the papers together after the press ran. We'd be there sometimes until 10 or 11 at night and occasionally after midnight when the press broke down. Though the hours weren't great, I enjoyed working hard and having spending money.

Senior Year: Work, Play, and Decisions

My senior year was the year that really lit things up. Thanks in a large part to Coach Charlie, we won the conference championship in football, the district championship in basketball and also in baseball. I was captain of the basketball and baseball teams and quarterback in football.

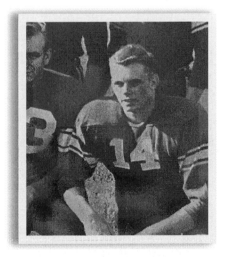

My final year at Jefferson Senior High School

Another life event happened that year: I started dating the girl who would later become my wife. Virginia Carlson was a part of the Girls of '62 and I had known and been friends with her since dating Marcy as a sophomore. She wasn't a cheerleader but was cute, blonde, and really smart. In fact, she was a leader in two school clubs. She was president of the math club and pep club. The pep club kept her connected to sports, which I really appreciated.

Virginia came from a good, stable Lutheran family and was the youngest of five siblings. Barbara was the oldest followed by Marilyn, Jim, David, and then Virginia. Her dad was a doctor with a small private practice in Alexandria. Virginia's mom, Charlie, had been a nurse, but by the time I knew her, she was a stay-at-home mom who devoted herself to her family and community. She was an extremely warm, caring, and open woman. Their house was always filled with friends, food, and fun and I always felt welcomed when I would go to dinner there. Virginia's mom and I became close that year. She was a real encouragement to me. She asked me about my life, school, and my family, just listening and making me feel special. We talked about what I wanted after I graduated high school. She encouraged me to pursue my dreams.

Dr. Carlson, Virginia's dad, was a quiet, steady man. He had good judgment and would give wise advice when asked. He was extremely polite. One time I joined them for Sunday dinner, and we sat down and started eating when Dr. Carlson said to me, "Help yourself to the butter." Well, I didn't want any, so I told him, "No, thank you." But I didn't know that was his way of asking for himself—*he* wanted the butter. Thankfully, his kids knew that and passed the butter to him. I noticed and got the hint.

We had plenty of good friends we hung out with regularly. Of course Virginia had the Girls of '62, and I had the guys on my sports teams. But there were a couple of others I got close to in high school, such as George Clifford. He lived close to Virginia's family and his dad was also a doctor. Dr. Carlson and Dr. Clifford even helped form the Alexandria Clinic, the largest medical clinic in Alexandria. George wasn't into sports but was a really good guy and I enjoyed hanging out with him as well as Bob Davis, Chuck Strandberg, and Frank Novak.

A couple times a month, Virginia and I would go dancing at either the Lakeside Pavilion in Glenwood or the New Munich Pavilion. There would be live bands and we'd dance and hang out afterward with our close group of friends. At the pavilions, they regularly had Bobby Vee, Bill Haley and the Comets, and other bands and performers. It was a lot of fun! Another thing that made my senior year one to remember was all the school dances. We'd often play football Friday night and have a dance Saturday night. Dancing was special to Virginia and me—even years later. In fact, I taught my daughter, Suzie, how to jitterbug as she grew up and we'd do the old-style dances in our living room.

Virginia and I at prom, 1962

My brother was just entering high school as I was leaving it. He did well in high school, always the clown, but he was also into sports—especially football, where he was a quarterback. Later in life, I learned about two common roles that emerge from the children of alcoholics: the hero and the clown. That's what Duane and I were. I was the perfectionist who wanted to bring positivity into the family. I did that by helping my mom as much as possible, excelling in sports, and making sure Duane stayed out of trouble. My brother was the clown. He would try to bring a lightheartedness to every situation. He found out he could also hide his woundedness behind his jokes and comedy.

We would see my Grandpa Vic and uncles Leroy and Vic Jr. on a regular basis. We mostly went to their house on Sundays for brunch. Grandpa and Uncle Leroy and Uncle Vic Jr. loved to play cards. Whist was their favorite Sunday game and they included me sometimes. The Minnesota Gophers from the University of Minnesota broadcasted their games on the radio, and it was also fun to listen to them at my grandpa's house. Little did I know that years later I would almost become the head football coach of the Gophers.

Grandpa had fought in WWI and then became a rural mail carrier. He was pretty serious, Norwegian by heritage and very calm but supportive. However, he would occasionally have some local friends over to play cards. That's when it got rowdy. They'd argue and yell at each other, "Why did you play that?" or "What a dumb move that was!" It was hilarious to watch.

Uncle Leroy was a reporter for the popular state farm and agriculture newspaper. Even though he wasn't the sports reporter, he was always interested in my games. As the years passed, I realized that I had a supportive network of relatives who helped me reach success, and I am extremely thankful.

The end of my amazing high school senior year was bittersweet. It was so nice to celebrate graduation with the seniors and be done with high school forever, but it was hard ending that winning year and saying goodbye to all my friends and especially Virginia, who would be heading off in the fall to a different college, four hours away. Virginia graduated magna cum laude, and I like to kid that I graduated "thank you laude."

That year I had decided to apply for college at Coach Charlie's alma mater, Concordia College in Moorhead, Minnesota, a city about 100 miles from Alexandria. Coach Charlie had arranged a visit from Coach Jake Christiansen, who came down and talked to a couple of my teammates and me. I didn't need to be convinced to attend the school. If Coach Charlie recommended the school, that was it. In the spring of my senior year, I was able to visit Concordia. The coaches showed us around the campus, and we met some players and saw the dorms and the athletic facilities. It got me excited to attend and play ball there.

Our 1961 championship football trophy at Jefferson Senior High

They ended up offering me a sports and academic scholarship and a work opportunity to play basketball, baseball, and football. This is unheard of today. I was so excited to be able to attend and not be a financial burden to my mom or rack up huge school loans. I enrolled with a major in physical education and a minor in biology because I wanted to be a coach like Coach Charlie and, back then, to be a coach, you had to teach classes too.

The summer between high school and college was mostly filled with work, baseball, and conditioning training to get me physically ready for college ball. My new coaches at Concordia had sent me some information about my college itinerary and some workout information. They were also just opening up a brand-new drive-in restaurant in Alexandria, the Orbit Drive-In. They had carhops—people pulled in and the gals would go out and take their orders.

My friend Bill Donelly and I were the assistant managers of the Orbit for that summer. Bill, who I played football with in high school and college, was a character. Somebody would come in and say, "This guy wants a rare hamburger," so Bill would only cook it on one side. Two of the girls who worked there were classmates of ours, Marilyn and Karen. We'd make them go down in the basement to clean the chicken. It was their job, but it was not a pleasant task and we made sure they did it because *we were the assistant managers.* We had many good laughs about that as the years went by.

When it was slow at the Orbit, Virginia would come by to hang out, but on weekends or evenings when the movie at the next door drive-in theater finished, everybody would drive over for food and then it was packed. I learned to stay focused and deal with unhappy customers when we were backed up.

Being an assistant manager at the drive-in restaurant taught me a lot of things. Because of sports, I knew how to motivate people, how to work hard, and how to be dependable. At the drive-in, I learned about customer service, how to deal with money and payments, and how to clean. By the end of the summer, I was a grease-cleaning expert.

My two summer baseball teams also kept me busy. I played American Legion and also played for the town team, the Alexandria Clippers. Between working, the two baseball teams, working out, and seeing my girlfriend, my summer flew by.

One thing that happened before heading to college was unforgettable. That summer I got to play against Satchel Paige, a really incredible baseball pitcher. After he was done in the majors, he formed an All-Star team, and they would come to various towns and play against the local All-Star teams. His All-Star team came to Alexandria and played against our team. Not only did I get to bat against Satchel Paige, but I went two for four that day. So I tell people my lifetime batting average against Satchel Paige is .500.

I ended that summer knowing big things were coming. I would have to step out on my own, make my own good decisions, and be the man I wanted to be. That future was both scary and exciting.

Off to College

When September rolled around, I was ready and excited to start my college life. All of my things were packed in my '56 red and white two-door hardtop Chevy Bel Air, as I said goodbye to my mom, brother, and Virginia. I was so excited the 100-mile drive northwest to Moorhead and Concordia College seemed to take forever.

When I arrived, I moved into the dorms on campus and started classes and practices. My roommate's name was Mike Wolfe, and we became good friends. The academics were much more challenging than high school, but the sports made up for it. I quickly found out that college sports were much more intense than high school sports and I loved it.

But the excitement and novelty of college life quickly wore off and I found myself homesick. Because home was 100 miles away, I couldn't just pop in on my mom and enjoy her company. Cafeteria food did not compare with home-cooked meals. I went home a few times that year, but not as often as I would have liked. It was also hard to be so far away from Virginia. Her college was over six hours away and though Alexandria was on the way to her college, we hardly ever visited home at the same time.

Two teammates from high school in Alexandria ended up attending Concordia with me, Bill Donley and Bob Davis. It was nice to have a couple friends right off the bat, but I didn't have a problem making more friends.

The head football coach for Concordia College was an amazing coach known as Coach Jake, or the Silver Fox. I remember being asked in 1996 to contribute to a book about Coach Jake Christensen. As I thought back on his influence and actions, what struck me most was his leadership, strength, unselfishness, and deep commitment to excellence, both in football and as a person. I remember his warmth, honesty, integrity, and personal drive. He was a great inspiration to me as I went through the coaching ranks.

At Concordia, the freshman football players had their own freshman team. I also played on the varsity team and had some freshman-only games as starting quarterback. We ended up winning all of our freshman games that year.

The very first varsity game I played in is seared into my memory. We were playing against Gustavus Adolphus College in Minnesota, where Virginia was attending. We went down to play at their college and of course she was in the stands watching the game. It was freezing that day. We didn't have enough capes, so along with another freshman, my friend Bill and I were huddled under one cape freezing to death.

From a distance, I heard Coach Jake yell, "Hall! Hall!"

I asked Bill, "Did he call my name?"

Bill said, "Yeah, you better get up there."

I was the passing quarterback and he wanted me to throw a certain pass. He told me the play, so I ran in and motioned the senior quarterback off the field. He was quite shocked, I am sure.

As Virginia saw me running out on the field, she nudged the people she was with and said, "That's my boyfriend."

The ball was snapped. I dropped back to pass. It was a designed pass, where the running back went out of the backfield and down the sideline, so I dropped back to pass and I threw it right where I thought he should be, except there was a 6'8" defensive end who reached up and snagged it right out of the air. Now he and another guy in front of him, a blocker, started coming right at me and there was nobody between us. But then, right before they got to me, they tripped over each other and fell directly at my feet.

That was my first experience playing varsity football in college. Virginia had to be wondering, "What in the world is going on there?" We ended up laughing about it later that day.

That first year at college I played baseball, basketball, and football. Unfortunately, it was too much for me to play three sports at the college level. By the end of the day, after all of my classes, my work duty of washing clothes, cleaning equipment, and practice for all three sports, I'd get back to my dorm and just crash. I couldn't stay awake. To focus on my preferred sports, I made the decision to drop basketball starting my sophomore year.

Besides occasionally calling Virginia on the phone and exchanging letters, I made the very long drive to Gustavus Adolphus College a couple of times that year to visit her. Another teammate, John Hovey, was "going" with a girl from Gustavus too, so he would join me, and we would stay the weekend.

Virginia was majoring in biology and teaching and enjoyed her classes. She had joined a band playing guitar and singing. It was a string quartet—like Peter, Paul, and Mary. Her roommate, Sharon Anderson, was also in the band and they have remained good friends along with Sharon's husband, Hans.

At the end of my freshman year, I returned to Alexandria for the summer. I played again on the town team. That summer I painted houses with a couple of my high school friends. We ended up painting a motel. It was nice to work with friends I hadn't seen in a while.

That summer I also found out that Coach Charlie had been recruited to coach at Concordia as the backfield coach. I was ecstatic to say the least—he would be my coach once again! To top it off, he also became head coach of hockey and baseball, so I'd get to work with him in baseball.

Coach Charlie had attended Concordia from 1946-1950 and married Coach Jake's daughter. Charlie was a Hall-of-Famer in football and baseball at Concordia and a revered alumnus.

As I look back now, I realize that whenever Charlie showed up, people won—in life and on the field.

I was so glad to have Coach Charlie back in my life. His encouraging words, joyful attitude, and constant smile made each practice so much better.

By my sophomore year, I'd grown used to being away from home. However, I had a harder time being away from Virginia. Our relationship had grown more serious over the summer and only seeing her every few months was tough, though we continued to connect by letter and occasionally by expensive long-distance phone calls.

My schedule that year was much easier to handle. Dropping basketball had been a good decision, even though I missed playing. I was able to keep up with my classes, practices, and work schedule, and didn't feel exhausted at the end of the day.

During my sophomore year, I also moved out of the campus dorms. I found a small basement apartment close to campus and moved in with two other guys. We shared chores and groceries, but because of the size of our apartment, we didn't have many friends over. It was nice having some freedom and not having to follow the strict rules of the dorm.

The year flew by and before I knew it, I was heading home for the summer and would be able to see Virginia almost every day for three solid months.

A New Chapter of Life

To make some money that summer, I got a job on a construction crew in Alexandria. It wasn't construction so much as a sod crew, picking up rocks off the road and throwing them into a truck. It was long and hot work, starting at 8 a.m. and ending around 5 p.m. When not working full time, I spent time with Virginia. We talked about all sorts of things like our families, the future, our friends, and what we were learning at college. She was really smart and funny, and I enjoyed talking to her.

One day, one of our normal conversations led to talking about marriage. We talked about how hard it had been that year, being so far away from each other. We talked about the possibility of getting married soon and her transferring colleges from Gustavus Adolphus College to Concordia College. She would miss her friends and quartet, but she thought it would be worth it.

We decided to go for it. I talked to her dad and bought her a ring. She and her mom quickly planned a small wedding. The evening before our wedding, Virginia's dad took me aside. I was unsure about what he wanted to say to me, but it ended up being kind of humorous: "Every man needs a good woman to point out their faults." I quickly chuckled and agreed. I think it was his way of saying he approved of our marriage. We got married that next day, a rainy August day at the end of the summer of 1964. We spent our honeymoon weekend in Brainerd, Minnesota—Paul Bunyan country. After the honeymoon, we went back to Alexandria to get ready to go to Concordia.

After packing up everything we could fit in my '56 Chevy, we took off for the 100-mile trip to Concordia. Around the halfway point, the car started making all sorts of strange noises. I pulled off the road and looked under the hood. I was not a mechanic and had no idea what was going on. With nothing to do but try to get to the next town, we got back in the car and puttered our way to Fergus Falls. Fortunately, we made it and found a garage. The mechanic checked it out and gave us the bad news: it was dead. Not sure what to do, we called Virginia's mom, who immediately hopped in her car with her collection of hundreds of dimes, which she graciously used to buy us a car from the dealership that was next to the garage. It was an old '55 Buick. We moved all of our stuff from the dead car to the new-to-us car and continued on our way.

We found a small apartment close to the college, and I got a job working evenings and non-game weekends at the local sporting goods store to help cover the bills. I would pick up the occasional odd job as well. Virginia's parents generously offered to keep paying for her college. Between their help and my various jobs, we were financially okay—not rich, but getting along.

Virginia fit in really well at Concordia. We became good friends with three other couples. Bob Davis from Alexandria had gotten married, and he and his wife lived in our apartment building.

Doug and Georgann Eckheart and Jim and Judi Herk lived close by as well. Jim would later become my assistant coach. We would get together and play cards and watch shows on our brand-new $6 TV that took about five minutes to warm up. All of us are still good friends to this day.

We had to work out our transportation because of my schedule, so I usually took the car early in the morning and Virginia would ride her bike to school. She rode on the side of a main thoroughfare for most of the way and would get whistled at by all the truck drivers. She found it amusing.

Around the time school started my junior year, we found out that Virginia was pregnant. It was quite a shock, but we adjusted and made a plan for Virginia to finish college on time, even with a newborn. I didn't have a lot of worries about becoming a father. My own dad had failed to be there for me, but I felt like I had a lot of other good examples from the coaches who'd spoken into my life, not just about sports, but about responsibility, character, and life. I vowed I would not follow the same path as my father.

One of those coaches who influenced me was Coach Jake Christensen. He was a soft-spoken man, but when he wanted something emphasized, he emphasized it well. He cared about the players. Coach Jake set the standard for the Concordia sports program for many years. His winning example challenged the other coaches to raise their game.

We drove to a lot of our away games because many were in the Twin Cities. Coach Jake had a big old Cadillac, and all the quarterbacks rode with him in the Cadillac to the games so he could talk to us about the game plan. We would drive down the day before and talk about game-related stuff the whole time. Of course, all the other players were on the bus and they were jealous because we got to drive to the game in a Cadillac. That was Jake's method of coaching the quarterbacks. He wanted to have his time with us. He was a hands-on mentor.

Coach Jake had a different way about him. He had coached a long time and he had trouble sometimes with people's names. He'd tell funny stories, and he'd get the names mixed up and laugh at himself about it. Even if he knew you, he'd say, "Okay, yeah . . . you, you, *you*." There were two guys on the team named Hoseth and Gorseth and he got their names mixed up all the time.

In the beginning of my junior season, Coach Jake was pessimistic about our prospects. "We should be fairly strong in the backfield. But we will be quite weak in the line. We don't have the beef up there that we had last year. Most of the players will have to double up." However, because of some really good coaching and my teammates' dedication, along with some good old-fashioned luck, that fall our football team made it to the NAIA National Championship game.

Going to the championship game in Augusta, Georgia, was my first experience on an airplane. We flew a chartered plane from Fargo-Moorhead to Georgia. I was all eyes as the plane took off, but soon my excitement and nervousness settled down and I enjoyed the three-hour flight, snacks, and view. We had a great itinerary of things to do and places to eat. It was a wonderful wrap to a great season. To get there, we'd won the Minnesota Intercollegiate Athletic Conference Championship and all of the playoff games.

In the championship game in Georgia, we tied with Sam Houston State, Texas. But we were okay with that because we had played our hearts out. After we got home and the polls came out, we found out we were ranked No. 1 in the final NAIA ratings. It was Coach Jake's first and only undefeated season at Concordia.

Playing football at Concordia

Baseball went pretty well that year too. I was one of the top hitters in the conference, percentagewise. We didn't win a championship, but we were good.

Life continued to fly by the rest of that school year. I stayed busy with school, practice, work, hanging out with friends, and taking care of Virginia. She continued in her classes as long as she could while getting plenty of rest. When she was close to her due date, she moved back in with her parents. Her dad was a doctor and her mom was a nurse, and they kept an eye on her and the baby. I continued at college and would visit when I could.

Our daughter was born on April 22, 1965, in the hospital in Alexandria. We named her Suzanne Marie Hall and called her Suzie or Suz. Both she and Virginia came through the labor healthy and without any problems. It was a monumental moment when Suzie was born.

Suzie as a newborn

Both of Suzie's grandmothers were so happy to have her and Virginia close by, at least for a few weeks. However, Virginia was anxious to take our daughter and join me at home in our apartment.

That summer we didn't move back to Alexandria. I got a job as a relief milkman driver. Jim Herk, one of my fellow football teammates, was also a relief driver and got me the summer job. We worked for Fairmont Foods and were hired to cover regular delivery-men's routes while they were on their two-week annual vacations.

To train us, we would ride with the regular driver for a week, learn the route, and then when the driver went on vacation, we took over their route.

The first driver I trained with told me, "If you see somebody new move into the neighborhood here on the route, load up the basket with some product and take it up to them as a gesture to see if they want to become a customer."

One day, I saw a gal out on her porch. I decided to try to make a customer for the company, so I loaded up my basket with eggs, cottage cheese, butter, chocolate milk, whole milk—lots of different things. I put them in the basket and jumped out of the truck in my white uniform with Fairmont Foods embroidered on it. Well, as I bounded up to the steps, I tripped on the stairs and spilled everything all over her front porch. It was a mess—eggs and cottage cheese everywhere. Feeling awful, I helped her clean it up and said, "Ma'am I am so sorry." Finally, after everything was cleaned up, I opened the screen door for her, and she went in. I closed the door after her and happened to catch my sleeve in the door and ripped my new uniform! I don't think she ever became a customer of Fairmont Foods.

The summer passed and we adjusted to having a newborn at home. I worked full time that summer and kept up my workouts and training for the fall football season. We looked for someone to help take care of Suzie while Virginia was in class. We were very grateful to find a lady with a young child in our apartment building who didn't mind helping out. Everything was set for our final year at college.

Senior Year

Senior year began and I was busy being a husband, father, student, quarterback, and breadwinner. However, because I had my sights set on coaching and needed the practice, I volunteered to coach and manage an intramural basketball team and did some refereeing during the basketball season.

My football and baseball teams had a good season, although they didn't make it to the championships. We didn't have a winning season like the year before, but we were close. St. John's College nicked us for the football playoffs. They were known as the Johnnys, the Catholics. We used to chant this prayer: "Hail Mary, Mother of Grace; put the Johnnys in second place."

Virginia took classes and found out she would be able to graduate the following summer. Due to the financial strain we were under, it was a big relief to know she would be done with her degree and be able to find a job teaching.

One door opened during my senior year that started me on a new path and would eventually change my perspective, mindset, and entire life. I took a confirmation class with the college chaplain, Pastor Lee. It was the beginning of a spiritual awakening for me, which didn't fully come to life until years later in Washington. But the class really awoke inside me a hunger to know more about God. That class led to years of thinking and talking about what I thought about God. Soon after the class started, I talked to Virginia and we decided that attending church regularly was important.

That year, I had a humorous, humbling event happen in baseball. I was leading the league in batting and we were playing in Minneapolis one day. A New York Yankee scout came to watch us. Before the game, the scout got our statistics, which made me look really good. Well, I proceeded to go up to the plate three times, swung nine times, and never touched the ball. That was the last I saw of a major league scout.

During the winter and spring of my senior year, I started looking around and applying for coaching jobs. I knew I would have to work in high schools until I got more experience, but my goal was to coach college football.

Fortunately one of the assistant coaches at Concordia, Jim Christopherson, who had been a kicker for the Vikings, knew of an opening at his old high school in Henning, Minnesota. Both the football and basketball coaching jobs were open because they were losing what they thought were all their great players in their big senior class and so the coaches were all leaving too.

Jim approached me and said, "Would you be interested in looking at this job at Henning where I played?"

I said, "Sure."

By my senior year, I had school debt of about 750 dollars, and I didn't have any idea how I was going to pay for it. It was causing me stress so I mentioned it to my mom. She must have mentioned it to my grandpa, because the next thing I knew, he had written a check for the entire amount. I felt humbled. My grandpa was generous. He was a quiet man but was there for you when you needed him. I was so thankful and resolved to be like him.

Grandpa Vic with Suzie

I graduated that spring and Virginia was able to finish up her last classes and graduate that summer. We had a small celebration with our close friends and family. It was a huge relief to be done. I was ready to move on.

High School Coaching at Henning

After Virginia had officially graduated, we packed up our apartment, loaded our car, and headed to Henning, Minnesota, where my coaching career began.

When I accepted the job at Henning High School, Virginia accepted a job teaching at a high school in a small town called Deer Creek, which was only about 15 minutes away. They needed a math teacher and they called the high school in Henning to see if they knew of anybody who could do the job. They knew Virginia was a teacher and good at math, and they recommended her. Deer Creek called her and offered her the job. She was a biology major but was willing to teach math. In fact, she comprised the entire Math Department.

At Henning, I coached with my former college football teammate and friend, Jim Herk. He was two years older and had been the defensive coach for the two years since he graduated. I came in as the head coach. We made a great team and are still best friends. Henning was my coaching launch pad.

The coaches prior to me left because they thought nobody was left in the cupboard. Thankfully there were a couple outstanding players left and with a bit of out-of-the-box thinking, our first year blew everyone out of the water. One of our outstanding players was a young man named Bob Bjorklund. Bob was my quarterback and the point guard on the basketball team as well. He was an amazing athlete who led us to championships. He later became an excellent college basketball coach and then the athletic director at Bethel University. He was one of the key ingredients for our team at

Henning. He was incredibly talented. The entire three years he was the quarterback of the Henning Hornets, we only lost one game. He was one of those players I remember very vividly. Two other players that made a tremendous difference were Gerald Brutlag and Stan Eckoff.

After arriving and taking inventory of our players, I realized we desperately needed a receiver and a guy to play center. I got one of the student managers to be a receiver and I went down to the woodshop to talk to the teacher about who was good with their hands. He told me about one of his students who excelled in the class. I convinced that student, who had never played football, to join us and I made him the center.

Though many people said it was impossible, we won every game that year.

Our winning Henning High School football team, 1968 (I am on the top right)

A lot of what I took from Concordia into my first job at Henning came from Coaches Jake and Charlie—their offense, their defense, and their caring about the players. When I got to Henning,

I was blessed to have a "playbook" already set up from those two incredible coaches, not just for football games, but for coaching and mentoring the football players in life. I already knew they were great young men ready for the challenge.

When you're coaching, you get players with all kinds of problems. They've got injury problems, girlfriend problems, and maybe even problems at home—especially in high school. There was a young sophomore named Randy Guse who was a tremendous athlete, well-built and fast. But Randy had Type 1 diabetes and his mom wouldn't let him play football. One day I sent a letter home with him and just shared my feelings about how joining the team could help him get a scholarship to college and how, because his health was under control, football would be good for him. He was just dying to play, too. She consented and he ended up being an All-State player and went on to Concordia College to become a tremendous football player.

Back then, you couldn't just coach; you had to teach classes too. So I taught eighth-grade science, health, and physical education. Soon after beginning teaching, I realized that teaching is coaching and coaching is teaching. They were very much the same. Both teachers and coaches spoke into students' minds and hearts. However, the practical aspects of teaching sometimes led to mishaps and fun memories.

In my eighth-grade science class one day, I was doing an experiment with a Bunsen burner. I turned on the gas to the burner, not realizing the burner had a leak. I explained to the class the experiment and then went to light the match to start the burner under the liquid. As you could imagine, the gas had leaked all around me. The moment I lit the match, the gas ignited. It was mayhem in the classroom. The girls in the front row started screaming and the class was in chaos. Thankfully, everything but my eyebrows were unscathed. It was quite the experience and I learned really quickly to not turn the gas on before I was ready.

I coached football and basketball, and then in the summer I was the summer recreation director for the kids and even drove the bus. I also managed the town baseball team. I was a player and manager.

Those first years I made $5,000 a year plus $600 for coaching. Virginia made $4,400. Between the two of us in 1966, we felt rich.

Virginia's first year of teaching was interesting. In her first semester teaching math, she flunked the principal's son. The principal didn't speak to her for about three weeks, but he soon realized his son deserved it and came to respect her for standing firm. The kid hadn't tried and was used to skating by because of his father. People gave him a free pass, but not Virginia. He got the F he earned.

When I asked her about it, she said, "He didn't pass any of his tests. He didn't try. So what was I to do?" Virginia ended up giving the principal's daughter a D minus. I was proud that she wasn't the kind of person to give in to pressure or conform to what wasn't right. And it definitely was a unique way to start her teaching career.

That year, she found out she really loved teaching, even with some challenging kids. She cared about the kids, was patient, and found fun ways to help them learn. She was a great teacher and her students loved her. After we moved, some of them would write to her, telling her how much they missed her.

While Virginia worked, we found a sitter to stay with Suzie. Suzie's grandmas were excited that we were in Henning, which was only 45 minutes away from them. They regularly took turns coming to visit.

After the first year, Virginia was able to transfer to Henning when a job opened up to teach math and science. It was nice to be at the same school and working with her.

During my three years at Henning, we only lost one football game. We went 8-0, 7-1, 8-0. I was named district Coach of the Year all three years. It was a huge honor. I had worked hard and done my best, but also knew the players, my fellow coaches, and God had played a huge part. It was a team deal and I loved those players.

The time we were in Henning was good for our family. We lived in a little home and were not strapped for money for the first time since getting married. Suzie grew and started to show a cute, fun little personality. She celebrated her second, third, and fourth birthdays in Henning. In fact, at the age of 4, Suzie had an opportunity to be a little princess on a float in the Fourth of July Parade and she absolutely loved it.

I really enjoyed coaching with Jim Herk. We had become good friends at Concordia and that friendship carried through to Henning. Virginia and I would get together with Jim and Judi once a week for games and dinner. We were both on a tight budget, so even if we had to have soup, we would do it together and have a good time. One of the funniest stories Jim tells about this time has to do with one of those get-togethers.

One evening Judi and I went over to Skip and Virginia's for dinner. Virginia was making spaghetti and we were really looking forward to it. It was after work and we were all pretty hungry.

Skip and I were hanging around, talking in their living room together, waiting for the sauce to get done when we hear a crash that sounded like glass breaking in the kitchen. We rushed in to see what had happened and if the women were all right. They were not hurt, but somehow a glass jar had fallen from the cupboard above the stove and landed on the edge of the spaghetti sauce pot, breaking into pieces with some falling into the sauce.

After getting the glass that had fallen outside the pot cleaned up, we discussed what we should do. On the one hand, eating glass was not a good idea. On the other hand, we were starving and didn't want to start over (or buy the ingredients all over again). We decided to get as much glass out as possible and then eat the spaghetti very, very carefully. We laughed about that for a long, long time.

Life Challenges

A couple of hard events marred my time at Henning. My mom called one evening in the winter of 1966/67. I had been teaching and coaching that day with no thought about the war that was raging on the other side of the world. Suzie was asleep in her little bed and Virginia and I were relaxing after a late dinner. I answered the phone and heard my mom's anxious voice, "Your brother just got drafted. He doesn't want to fight and is thinking about going to Canada." I knew this had been a possibility but didn't think it would ever happen.

After Duane graduated from high school, he had gotten a job working at a construction company. He was the right age for service in the military, not too tall or short, healthy and fit. I couldn't think of a way for him to be excused from serving. Nothing came to mind. Duane had been such a happy kid. He was funny—a prankster. I worried that war would take that from him. I asked to talk to him. I encouraged him not to go to Canada. He could get in a lot of trouble doing that. I told him I would be there for him. He could do this.

Over the next couple of months, he got his physical and headed off to bootcamp and training. During his R&R before shipping out to Vietnam, Virginia and I were able to see him and say a hard goodbye. My baby brother was going to war.

One other hard thing happened while we were in Henning. My grandpa passed away during the third year. It was a sad loss for us. I was grateful to be close enough to go to the service and support my mom and uncles. I didn't realize until he was gone what a solid pillar he had been in my life. He wasn't demonstrative, but he had always been there for me, Duane, and my mom.

Even though we had such successful football seasons and a good solid family foundation, I started thinking about going back to college and getting my master's degree and becoming a college football coach. It had always been my desire and I was ready to continue the pursuit of my vision. I discussed it with Virginia, and she was supportive as always. During my third and final year at Henning High School, I applied to the master's programs at four universities: Arizona, Arizona State, Colorado, and Colorado State.

Initially, I received an offer from Arizona. But then the University of Colorado accepted me and there was no turning that down because it was a Big 8 football school. I had to decline the Arizona offer to go to Colorado. And then Mike Lude, who I would later work with, called from Colorado State, but because I had already accepted the University of Colorado, I turned him down but would join him later at Kent State. I was headed to the University of Colorado in Boulder, Colorado and big time football.

Virginia's senior photo

My senior photo

◄ 4 ►

Off to University of Colorado

The summer of 1969 came, and Virginia and I packed up Suzie and our home and made our way to Colorado for the University of Colorado's master's and football assistantship program. We found a small apartment in married student housing and I looked around for a part-time job.

After arriving, I taught several physical education classes like tennis and racquetball at the university, and a class in one of the local junior high schools. My own master's classes were scattered throughout the day, so I stayed pretty busy. But my top goal was to dive headfirst into college coaching.

The head football coach at Colorado was Eddie Crowder, who had played and coached at Oklahoma under Coach Bud Wilkinson. Don James was the defensive coordinator. Both of these men were legends to me. Coach Crowder had a quiet way about him. He didn't stomp or yell at his coaches or players. He kept his voice even and inspired his team to give their all.

Coach James was a smaller man with a large presence. He was really hands-on with those under him and we learned a lot. You could tell he really cared for the other coaches, players, and the game.

He had high, demanding standards and took everyone around him to the next level.

That first year, I also worked with a coach named Rick Duval, coaching the receivers. He was a good mentor to me. Rick and I had recruited a guy from a junior college named Cliff Branch Jr. He had great potential because he was really fast. In fact, while in college he won the NCAA Championship for the 100 meters. Unfortunately, he couldn't catch a thing, especially a football. After every practice that summer and fall, I had to stay late and throw 100 passes to Cliff. At the beginning, he probably dropped about 90 of them. Pretty soon he started catching on. He eventually became a fabulous punt returner as well as a dynamite receiver. He went on to play in the NFL for 14 years and won three Super Bowls with the Oakland Raiders.

It was with this group of coaches that I got the name "Skip." At one of our meetings, Jim Mora Sr. was at the chalk board, writing down the assignments—who would be responsible for the playbook, who would be responsible for each section, and so on. Of course, my name is Merle, but he could never spell Merle. He would put down M-U-R-I-L-L and I would say, "No, no that that's not right." Finally, he got so frustrated he said, "You need a new name. Something simple. SKIP! That's it."

And that is how I got the name Skip.

The rest of the year at Colorado flew by. We found out Virginia was pregnant with our second child early in the spring of 1970. I was excited, but hardly had time to think about it with all of my school, family, teaching, and coaching responsibilities.

It was during this time that I was offered two coaching opportunities, one at a small college and one at a large high school. They were tempting, but ultimately I stayed focused on my college coaching vision and that kept me on the path to finishing my postgraduate degree.

University of Colorado Buffalo Brain Trust

Our Family Is Complete

In the middle of the summer between my first and second year at the University of Colorado Boulder, Christopher Scott Hall was born. On August 5, 1970, I was teaching a summer women's tennis class with mostly housewives. That day somebody came rushing out to the park where we were doing the tennis class. They said, "Virginia is in the hospital! She's ready to deliver!"

Of course, all these housewives said, "You got to go! You got to go!" They basically escorted me to the car.

I got out of there and headed to the hospital. I made it to the delivery room on time. The nurse helping Virginia kept listening to the baby's heartbeat and because it was going fast, she predicted it was going to be a little girl.

Well Chris came out and they held him up and I said, "Doesn't look like a girl to me!" Both Virginia and I were thrilled to have a boy. I originally wanted to name him Mickey after the great Mickey Mantle, but Virginia wasn't having it. After some discussion, we decided to name him Christopher and call him Chris for short.

Having two kids was a bit of a transition, but Suzie adored Chris and was really helpful. I had heard it can be hard on the first child when another comes along, but we didn't have any trouble. She loved him as much as we did. Because everything was smooth at home, I felt good about being able to focus on my studies and dive into that next football season as a second-year graduate assistant coach.

I completed my master's coursework by the end of football season that first year. I decided to do my master's thesis on *The Theory of Coaching*. I began writing it once the season wrapped up.

Featured in Sports Illustrated

My first year at Colorado, the team played really well. At the start of the season, we were ranked #18 in the AP Poll. Our second game was against #4 Penn State, who had a 23-game winning (and 31-game undefeated) streak. Though we had won our first game and were fired up to face Penn State at home, it was still daunting. However, we had a powerhouse of talent on our team including four players who went on to play in the NFL: Herb Orvis, who played for the Detroit Lions and the Baltimore Colts; Rick Ogle, who played for the St. Louis Cardinals and the Detroit Lions; John Tarver, who played for the New England Patriots and the Philadelphia Eagles; and Ward Walsh, who played for the Houston Oilers and Green Bay Packers. We had another great player named Bobby Anderson and also had a unique player who was a safety and punter named John "Bad Dude" Stearns. After college, Bad Dude was a 17-round pick by the Buffalo Bills *and* a second overall pick in the Major League Baseball draft by the Philadelphia Phillies. He ended up choosing baseball.

When our team faced the daunting Penn State, we did our best and beat them 41-13 during a crazy winter snowstorm. We were elated. That following week, we were thrilled to be featured on the cover of *Sports Illustrated* with a detailed article about how we dominated the game.

Though the Colorado Buffs were doing really well the first year we were at Colorado Boulder, and though I was enjoying being a part of that great university, money was weighing heavy on my mind and the little I was bringing in didn't go very far. Because of the stress about finances, I started thinking about looking for a full-time coaching position at a good-sized high school, hoping that would be my next step to college coaching.

In late spring of my first year at Colorado, I heard about a large, well-known high school in Littleton, Colorado, that was looking for a head football coach. I couldn't pass it up, so I headed down there to interview. After a really good interview, they offered me the job. The school had such a great football program that the position even included a house. It was going to be a huge step up financially, which was a relief to both Virginia and me.

After I accepted the job, I got back to the University football office and Big Jim Mora, one of the assistant coaches, was there. I said, "Hey Jim, I just got offered a job at Littleton High School."

He replied, "High school? I thought you wanted to be a college coach."

I hesitated, then answered, "I do."

He asked, "Then what are you taking that job for?"

Well, that question hit me like a middle linebacker.

After I got home, I talked to Virginia about my dilemma. On the one hand, the high school job was at a very large high school with a great football program and good money. On the other hand, my vision was to coach college ball. Should I settle for what was before me, or hold out for what I wanted? We decided to go for the ultimate goal and stay the course.

The second season for the Colorado Buffs was up and down. We won as many as we lost but still ended up making it to another Liberty Bowl against Tulane. Unfortunately, we lost 7-15.

Coach Don James was an up-and-coming potential head coach. He was the defensive coordinator at Colorado and a lot of universities had been looking at him. Earlier that year he had called me into his office and wanted to know what my goals were, what I wanted to do with my life. I told him in no uncertain terms, "I want to coach college football."

That fall he finally settled on taking the Kent State Head Coach position in Ohio and was looking at who would be on his coaching staff at the new college. In December, a few weeks after the bowl game, I got a call from Don. He said, "Skip, I'd like to have you on my staff at Kent State." He offered to start me off as the head freshman coach, a varsity assistant, and also coaching the offensive backfield.

I replied, "That's great, Coach. When do you want me there?"

He answered, "Yesterday." That was the Don James timetable.

I went home in a daze and told Virginia. She was excited too. She had been my biggest supporter on my quest to coach college football. It wouldn't have happened if I had settled and taken the high school coaching position. But because we held on to our vision of coaching college football, I was now going to be a full-time college coach.

My head was spinning with all the logistics that needed to happen before I got to coach. I still had my thesis to finish and then I needed to defend it before I would be done with my post-graduate degree. I set up a schedule to get it done that spring and set a date to return to Colorado to defend it. Once all of that scheduling was done, we packed our house, loaded the U-Haul, and headed to Ohio.

◄ 5 ►

Overcoming the Odds at Kent State

Coming into Kent State as a full-time college coach was hard. In my first five years of coaching—three in high school and two at Colorado Boulder—we had won three championships and been to two bowl games. At Kent State my first year, we finished dead last in the conference.

Head coach Don James wanted to change all that for the players, the fans, the coaches, the university, and the whole community. We had a pretty aggressive off-season workout program. Due to the work and hardships involved, we lost some of the less-than-committed Kent State Golden Flashes football players. We looked at that as a positive thing. We were able to trim the guys who would hold the football program back. Bad attitudes from established players about the new coach and new staff can become a cancer you certainly don't want on a team.

During my first spring at Kent State, we recruited so well that we had a tremendous quarterback and a tremendous tailback. I recruited a quarterback named Greg Kokal from Cleveland. He played as a freshman after the starting quarterback was injured. Greg was the spark who really got us going. He had another three outstanding years and ended up getting picked in the 11th round in the NFL draft.

The original James Gang coaching staff at Kent State

Larry Poole was a tremendous tailback who had been recruited by a lot of other schools, but we got him. He later got drafted in the ninth round by the Cleveland Browns. Those two guys were a one-two punch.

We also had some good linemen such as Walt Vrabel. We also recruited a young man from a junior college named Gerald Tinker who was lightning fast. I timed him in the 40-yard dash at 4.15 seconds. I had to look at my stopwatch twice. I couldn't believe it. I had never had anyone that fast on a team. It came as no surprise to me that while at Kent State, he competed in the 1972 Olympics. His team won a gold medal in the 4x100 relay. After college, he was drafted by the NFL and played for the Atlanta Falcons and then the Green Bay Packers.

We had a few more incredible players: Jack Lambert, who went on to play for the Pittsburgh Steelers and win four Super Bowls. We also had Gary Pinkel, who joined our coaching staff and then went on to be head coach at Toledo and then Missouri. One other instrumental player was Tom Bucheit, who was captain of our '74 team.

One of the most famous coaches came out of this amazing team. Many people don't realize the legendary coach Nick Saban was a defensive star and played at Kent State while I was there. He also began his coaching career there. He had planned to go back home and take over the operations of the family business after college, but decided to stay so his wife, who was a year behind him, could finish college. Coach James heard he was going to stay and talked him into joining the coaching staff as a graduate assistant. He did, discovered he loved coaching, and the rest is history.

We were slowly building an incredible college football team, but it couldn't happen fast enough. I spent most of that spring recruiting. All of the coaches did. We each had an assigned region. My area was the country club side of Cleveland, and I brought in quite a few that first year—eight or nine. Because some guys had quit, we had a lot of scholarships available.

Upset in America and My Family

Recruiting for Kent State was not easy. It was a good state college, not fancy, but solid. Unfortunately, in the spring before I arrived, a violent event had shaken America to its core: the Kent State Riots. The entire national fiasco started when President Nixon ordered an invasion of Cambodia instead of continuing to withdraw American troops as promised. Americans found out and protests erupted around the country and on most college campuses. Kent State was no different in 1970. To this day, it's been difficult for Kent State to shake that incident from the minds of those who were alive at that point in history.

On Saturday, two days before the nation-altering event, student protesters set fire to the ROTC building on campus and harassed the fire department when they showed up to put it out. The next day was calm, but on Monday, May 4, 1970, a large, organized group of students got together to protest the Vietnam War and the president's actions. The local police had called in the National Guard two days before and more than 100 guardsmen were present on campus, milling around with their M1 military rifles.

On the fateful day, close to 3,000 students showed up in front of the burned-out ROTC building with posters and rocks. The student protesters were forcefully dispersed, and they retaliated by throwing rocks. Some guardsmen got caught between the football field fencing and the angry, rock-throwing crowd. Twenty-eight guardsmen ended up firing their weapons, some into the air and some into the crowd. Four students were killed and nine injured. Following the shooting, the university was ordered closed and remained shut down for six weeks.

Virginia and I showed up seven months after that event and the school, staff, students, and leaders were still recovering. The entire state of Ohio was wary about the event, the school, and the students. Parents were not easily convinced to send their sons to play football in the very school where such a huge tragedy had just occurred.

The Vietnam War was having an impact not only on the country, the state, and the colleges, but on my family as well. I received regular updates from my mom on how Duane was doing. She called one day saying he had been injured. His half-track had driven over a landmine and exploded. Most of his platoon died and he was severely burned, his elbow was shattered, and he had shrapnel in his leg. They were stabilizing him and flying him home as soon as possible.

My mom was devastated. She had been afraid something like this would happen. He'd have a long road to recovery. I was shocked and saddened too. Virginia and I were worried about him. We hoped he would be able to come home soon.

When Duane was finally shipped home, he ended up in a burn hospital in Texas. My mom flew to be with him and only then did she find out the extent of his injuries. He had burns on over 40 percent of his body and had almost died because of a pulmonary infarction. He pulled through, though some shrapnel still remains in his body. With his experiences and injuries came emotional trauma as well. Vietnam had changed him.

He spent quite a few months in Texas and when he had recovered enough to leave the hospital, he was discharged from the Army. He moved in with my mom, who was living in Seattle. She was able to help him get back on his feet and as soon as he was able, he enrolled in college at Western Washington in Bellingham. When I talked to him on the phone, I could tell that the fun-loving young man was gone. In his place was a serious, scarred soldier. I hoped as time went on that his carefree attitude would come back or at least that he could find some peace.

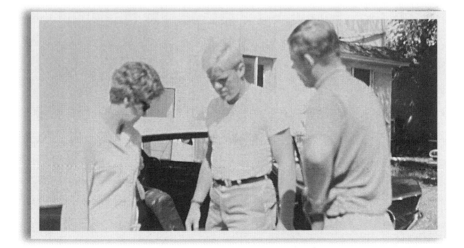

Mom and I saying a hard goodbye to Duane as he
headed off to Army boot camp

Recruiting for Kent State After the Riots

The war and the incident at Kent State had long-term effects on football recruiting. That first year, I remember recruiting a guy who really wanted to play at Kent State. We would have loved to have him on our team. When I went to his house to talk to him and his parents, his mom thought we had guns under our coats. She viewed us as a threat. She shut us down and sent us packing.

For recruiting purposes, we each had an assigned geographical area we were responsible for. We canvased all the high schools in our area and talked to the high school coaches, asking them who they would recommend to become a college player.

We would get recommendations and then collect film on those candidates. The film came in big reels inside cans. We hauled those big cans of film around and watched them together to do our evaluations. If it was a defensive player, the defensive coaches all evaluated the player together.

Likewise, offensive players were evaluated by the offensive coaches. While we watched the film, we graded the recruits. Don James had a tremendous system for putting it all together with grades. There were 10 tough questions we had to ask the high school coaches.

These questions began with this list:

1) Is this young man dying to be a great college football player?

2) Would he come early and stay late to practices to improve?

3) Was he interested in academics?

Most questions were about motivation and character. All these qualities were important to us. The high school coach's answers would give us a one through five ranking. At that point, we had to fill out the evaluation based on performance from the film we had watched. Lastly, we would ask for some general comments from the principal or advisors.

After all of this information was compiled, we presented a player to the full staff with a composite rating from all of the evaluations. If a player was a three, he was not one of the top choices . . . but if he was a four or a five, we offered some kind of scholarship, hoping we could entice him to play for us.

Once we went through all the nominations, recommendations, film evaluations, and all the tough questions, we would narrow it down. We might look at a hundred students and end up recruiting ten players. Evaluation is the key to successful recruiting.

Once we decided on a player and they passed the coaches' evaluation, I would set up a home visit to sit down with him and his family. We'd get to know each other and then we would organize a campus visit with the player and his family. During those visits, we had itineraries for each player laid out, campus tours, and meetings with professors of subjects they were interested in within their intended major.

We gave each visiting recruit a host player for their weekend visit, and they had the chance to get to know the player as much as they possibly could. These seasoned players were very important in the recruiting process because the recruits wanted to hear what the players had to say about the program and their complete experience with school and football. After the visit, if the recruit was still in the running for a scholarship spot, I would take Coach James back to the student's home for a second home visit where he laid out the whole program for the player and his parents.

This whole process took a large number of appointments, traveling, and phone calls. In those days, if we wanted to make a phone call to a player, we had to stop at a pay phone. We didn't have cell phones, so it was a lot of work, but we were very successful. Ohio is a hotbed for high school football, so we didn't have to go all over the place looking for players.

Amazingly, despite the rigorous standards and the school reputation from the riots, we had a great recruiting year. Parents and students must have seen something they really liked. We had to work hard at it, but we ended up with a solid group of football players. Unfortunately, as freshman, they just didn't have a ton of experience. Though we had an excellent training schedule and we saw improvements as the year went by, we ended our first season at Kent State dead last in the conference. We were so proud of our players and knew this would be a huge discouragement for them, like it was for us. We determined to fight even harder next season.

We continued our serious recruiting style that second spring in 1972. We found more amazing high school seniors and brought them into our program. We started looking at the lineup for our football team and began to get cautiously excited.

Football training began in earnest that summer. Coach James kept his rigorous training schedule and expected all team members to follow it. We all felt the pressure to have a winning football season. It was Coach James' second season, and the school was still recovering emotionally from the riots. Morale was at an all-time low and all eyes were on our football team.

Our very first game that season was against the University of Akron and though our players played well, we ended the game tied 13-13. Our second game was played against Louisville and we suffered a devastating loss, 34 to 0. I kept having flashbacks from the previous year and praying it would not be repeated.

We won the next game but lost two more in a row. Our team was consistent and hardworking but had just enough slip-ups to keep us from winning. Coach James would rally and inspire us weekly with his encouraging speeches. I was proud of our players and my fellow coaches. After our initial 1-3-1 record, we started winning. Our young men upped their game, gained confidence, and beat Bowling Green, Miami, and Toledo.

From Last in the Conference to the Tangerine Bowl

Due to the dedication and hard work of our players and coaches, that year we made it to the Tangerine Bowl against Tampa. This was not only a huge accomplishment, since we were dead last in the conference the year before, but also a much-needed morale boost to the team, Kent State University, and the whole community.

The Tangerine Bowl was in Orlando, Florida. It later became known as the Citrus Bowl. The Kent State players and coaches were having a hard time in Florida because news reporters were all over the place. They didn't want to know about us, football, or how we made it to the Tangerine Bowl. All they wanted to ask us about was the Kent State shootings that had happened two years prior to this season. It was hard on coaches and players and overall very discouraging.

The kickoff time on game day was 8 p.m., and we were told later that our game had the biggest crowd up to that point with 20,072 attendees. At the time, all I knew was the crowd was overwhelming, emotions were running high, and this game felt like a make-it-or-break-it moment for Kent State football.

Tampa had a huge 6'8" player named John Matuszak, who later went on to become a movie actor in the 80s. His most famous role was playing Sloth in the movie *The Goonies*. At the time he was a tough, mean, ornery football player when Jack Lambert met him on the field as team captains. Lambert, who was missing his two front teeth, scowled at Matuszak and in response, Matuszak took his helmet off and banged it on his head to show his toughness.

Despite this display of competitiveness, the game did not start out well for us. The Spartans shut us out of both the first and second quarter. We also suffered two intercepted passes that led to the Spartans second and third touchdowns. All of this happened before halftime.

At halftime, discouraged and exhausted, we regrouped in the locker room. Interestingly, I got up close and personal with a few famous characters. The coaches had their players separated into certain sections of the locker room. I had my players in one section trying to talk about something serious, and right next to them were Mickey Mouse, Minnie Mouse, Donald Duck, Goofy, and Pluto waiting to go out and be in the half-time show.

Coach James was not at all distracted by our strange guests. He took one look at the beleaguered players and coaches and decided something needed to change. He gave us one of his famous speeches. The man had a gift. He encouraged and exhorted us, convincing all of us we could do it. He told us the adversity we were experiencing would not break us; it would only make us stronger. Every man in that smelly room started the second half of the game with renewed purpose and a sense that no matter the current score (21-0), a win was still possible.

We got our first touchdown straight out of the gate when our quarterback, Greg Kokal, passed to Gerald Tinker. Our defense also upped their game and shut down Tampa from scoring at all in the second half. In the fourth quarter, we were able to get two more touchdowns but ran out of time to get a third, which would have put us ahead of the Spartans. We lost 21-18, but we were so proud of our team for not only getting us to the championship, but also recovering in the second half. The game later became known as "one of the sport's great hindsight games." Nobody thought much of it at the time, besides all the Kent State fans, but afterward, nobody could stop talking about it. It's been featured in multiple articles over the years and in books about incredible football games. It is also the only season Kent State has ever won the championship.

We came home to a supportive community that rallied around us. Things were looking up for Kent State.

The James Gang

After our second football season, all the coaches continued our heavy recruiting. Our schedule was almost as busy during recruiting season as it was during football season. One of the ways we let off some steam was at a restaurant called 11th Frame. We would come back from recruiting and get together in the lounge at the 11th Frame. Typically, at least three of us from the coaching staff—Bob Stull, Ray Dorr, and myself—would get a table and talk recruiting and everything football. The restaurant's owner, Dave, was a big Kent State fan. He'd see us come in and say, "Set the boys up! Set the boys up!" They'd bring us beers and we'd talk into the wee hours.

Our wives got annoyed with the amount of time we spent at the 11th Frame. We used to joke that if it ever burned down, we'd know who to blame. NFL scouts came to town regularly and they would wine and dine us, but not at the 11th Frame. That was the coaches' hangout.

Our family featured in a newspaper at Kent State

Because of the hectic schedule throughout the year, each coach got two weeks off in the summer. Virginia and I would take Suzie and Chris to different fun places in Ohio and then spend some time in Minnesota, visiting family and friends. We still have two cousins living in Alexandria, Lee and Al Edenloff. We would rent a cottage near their property on Lake Ida. The time was always filled with fishing and other water activities with the cousins.

Virginia started teaching again while we were at Kent State. She had earned her Ohio teaching certificate within the first year after we moved there and then found a job teaching science, which was her real passion. Her school was just outside of Kent.

Suzie started kindergarten our first fall in Kent. By the time Virginia started teaching full time, Suzie was in first grade and going to school all day. However, because Chris was still a baby, we found a reliable babysitter to watch him while Virginia taught school.

Coach James started the season of 1973 by talking to me about moving my coaching position. He wanted me to be a linebacker coach. He thought it would help prepare me to be a head coach someday. I agreed.

That season was a good one for football at Kent State. We didn't win the championship that year, but we did well with a 9-2 record. Then in 1974, people really started taking notice of Don James and his program because it was so well organized and recruiting was phenomenal.

After his third year, Coach James was recruited to Florida State as a potential head coach. He met with us before he went down there. He said, "Well, if I take this job, here's what'll happen—each of you will get a country club membership, cars . . . " We looked forward to the potential perks.

He had a really good interview. Once he came back, he got a phone call. They said, "We'd like to have you come back one more time."

He replied, "You know all about me; if you want me, take me now or I'm not interested." He didn't go. That ended up being a good thing, because after the next year, we ended up going to University of Washington.

In 1974, the head coach of the University of Washington, Jim Owens, announced he was going to retire. Dan Devine initially accepted the job, but then on his way to Washington, Notre Dame called and he turned around and headed there, and that opened the door for Don James.

Coach James flew out to Washington to see if it would be a good fit for him. When he came back after accepting the job, he called all of the assistants in one by one and talked to us about what he wanted and if he saw us fitting into his program at UW. He ended up taking four of us with him.

The rest of the coaches stayed at Kent State. One became the head coach, Dennis Fitzgerald. The others stayed on as assistant coaches, and Nick Saban was promoted to a full-time assistant for the next season.

The five of us—Coach James, Bob Stull, Ray Dorr, Dick Scesniak, and I—flew on Christmas Eve from Cleveland to Seattle. There was a big reception when we got there. It felt like a new beginning, hitting Seattle and the Husky faithful.

6

Joining the Huskies at UW

The former coach of the University of Washington, Jim Owens, was a classy guy. He had a good run at UW, ending his 18-year career in 1974 at 99-82. He was ready to retire. They had a couple of really down seasons and also had more than five years of racial unrest. A few years before we arrived, the Black Students Union at the University of Washington started a protest campaign, demanding that UW break all athletic connections with Brigham Young University, which was viewed as racist because of teachings in the Mormon Church at that time. They joined other black students at other universities that rallied and called for a ban against BYU. The protests at UW were much more militant than at other colleges and they would occasionally get violent, destroying sports equipment and threatening players. I think all of that finally got to Coach Owens and he was glad to be retiring.

Jim met our plane when we came in. He welcomed us and answered our questions. This type of hosting from a former head coach doesn't often happen.

We all stayed in a hotel right near the UW campus, the University Towers in Seattle, until our wives and kids came out to join us. Whenever a major transition like this happens, the coaching staff has to hit the ground running.

I was out there for a few weeks before Virginia came out with the kids. I even had to find a house to buy without her seeing it. A Realtor, Larry Jassen, connected with me and showed me a few houses that fit within our criteria. Virginia and I were looking for three bedrooms with an office and a roomy backyard where the kids could play. I mailed pictures of different homes to her through the process, and she would call me and tell me what she thought about the houses. Between my busy transition process and must-move-quickly recruiting schedule, we were able to find the perfect little house, a split level with a nice yard and an extra-long driveway. The price was just right at $36,500. We were official homeowners for the first time.

Since I was already in Seattle, Virginia was left with the logistics of wrapping up our rental home in Kent as well as taking care of the two kids. Thankfully, the University of Washington hired movers to load and move our stuff. Then Virginia got the two kids packed into the car and drove to her parents' house in Minnesota for a couple of days. Unfortunately, Suzie had a bad case of strep throat, so after Virginia's dad, Dr. Carlson, had treated Suzie, Virginia's Aunt Alice volunteered to help them finish the drive out to Seattle. It took a few days, but they made it to Montana just in time to get stuck in the middle of a huge blizzard.

I was sitting in my office overlooking Lake Washington on a nice sunny day in Seattle when my phone rang. I had barely picked up the receiver when I heard Virginia say, "I'm selling the car and we're flying!" It turns out she had just been on her back in the snow, under our new Oldsmobile sedan, putting on winter snow chains. It was something I'm sure she never wanted to experience. I felt bad for her and told her to just stay where she was, find a cozy hotel, and hunker down until the blizzard was over and the roads cleared. Later, when we could laugh about it, I told her I was going to have those chains bronzed and a special football wife trophy made for her. Coaches' wives are definitely MVPs.

Seattle was unlike anything we had experienced prior. Our house was in Redmond, Washington, by Lake Sammamish. It was an 11-mile drive to UW and I had to cross a floating toll bridge. Sometimes the toll booths would get really backed up, so we had a trick. There were a few of us who lived on the east side of the bridge. We would carpool as often as possible and the rule was that if there were three people in a car, you could go right on through the tolls in the right lane and not have to wait in traffic. Because of this situation, most of the time at least three coaches drove to the UW campus together. And if there were only two, we'd put up a mannequin in the backseat so we could go right on through and not be late.

Don James had a particularity about lateness: if you were 10 minutes early for the meetings, you were almost late. He was extremely punctual, organized, and detailed. It's what made him so good—everybody, coaches and players, understood their exact responsibilities. There was no guesswork. If you didn't do what you were supposed to do, Coach James didn't have to say much. He had "The Look." If you got "The Look," you knew you had better shape up.

The Don James Schedule

A coach's work schedule is pretty challenging and under Don James it was also methodical and organized, which made it very effective. We were usually on campus by 7 a.m. and ready for our first meeting at 7:30 a.m. We'd start with a staff meeting where all the coaches would go through their position players and give a report on each of them one by one.

For those of you who don't live and breathe football, every team is segmented into quarterbacks, running backs, receivers, offensive line, defensive line, linebackers, defensive backfield, kickers, etc. Each position had a coach that was an expert and could organize and instruct the players in their role. Those coaches met to create a game plan that would be presented to Coach James for approval and then implemented during practice along with the injury report from our trainer, Dennis Sealey.

Coach James would have his comments from the previous day's practice. He was mostly up in a tower, overlooking everything, taking meticulous notes. Coach James would go over all his notes and then we'd break up and work on offense and defense, starting to put the game plans together. We also set practice plans for the day. These meetings usually went from 7:30-9:00 a.m. After that, the offense and defense coaches would meet separately. Those meetings lasted a couple hours or more. Then we'd break for lunch. In the afternoon, we'd have meetings with the players—individual meetings and position meetings.

Coach James believed it wasn't good to drag things out. In fact, in position meetings, he didn't want us to meet with the players more than 30 minutes. Because most players started losing interest after 30 minutes, we needed to be sharp in our presentations. We looked at the previous day's practice and critiqued it for the individual as well as the team play. We used Coach James' critiques and also the film from the games and practices. The whole purpose was to get better and better.

In the afternoons before practice, I would meet with the academic counselor, Gertrude Peoples, to talk about any issues the players might be having with their schoolwork. I then shared that with the whole staff the next morning. If it was serious, position coaches would get involved and walk the players through their academic issues.

After individual and position meetings, practice would start. We always practiced in the afternoon after the players were done with their classes. During practice, everything was scripted—every play, every defense was on paper and that's what we followed in practice. Drills and everything else were separate, but when we worked with the team, everything was scripted. The practices were usually planned for two hours.

During practice, every coach had a script. Plays and defenses were called from the script. All the coaches worked to put the script together. The graduate assistant would write it up and print it out before handing these to each coach before practice.

One of the ways of getting and giving feedback to the players was through assessment of the games and practices. All practices and games were filmed and critiqued for strengths and weaknesses. Every player then received a grade on every play he participated in. The player would get a percentage grade. We were looking for 90 percent or above. If the player received a grade lower than 90 percent, we had some concern. If it was *way* below that, then we had a lot of work to do.

After practice, the coaches would have dinner and then we'd come back together. Coach James would join us at this point to go over offense and defense. We'd start looking at the film of the opponent for the coming week's game. Coach James had been mainly a defensive coordinator before becoming a head coach, so most of his time was spent with the defensive staff.

He would come in and we'd watch the film of the opponent for the week and critique it. We'd give ideas on what we should do and what kind of defenses we wanted to run. The coaches would each go to the board and write some ideas and thoughts they had and then Coach James would give his input too and we'd put a game plan together.

After that meeting, we'd be done for the day and get home around 10 at night. The next morning would start the same schedule all over again. It was a very effective plan and success was inevitable. This consistent, hard work was the price we paid for excellence. Champions are made in the details and with Coach James, we always focused on the details.

Every Thursday, Coach James gave a speech to the coaches and players. Over the years of working under him, I heard more than 200 weekly speeches. Every speech was different and unique in focus. The speeches impacted coaches and players alike, not just from a football standpoint but from a life perspective. He spoke about leadership, character, and other traits, and used examples from lessons he had learned firsthand as well as from the books he was constantly reading.

Years later, one of our former players, Pete Tormey, approached Coach James about his speeches. He asked if Coach James kept all of them. When he found out that every one of them had been saved, Pete asked, "Could I possibly write a book on these?" So Coach handed all of the Thursday speeches he had given at UW over to Pete, who turned them into a book that I highly recommend, called *The Thursday Speeches: Lessons in Life, Leadership, and Football from Coach Don James*. In this book, Pete wrote,

> *Don believed strongly in the power of education to transform lives. He believed that education was a lifelong process and, as The* Thursday Speeches *demonstrates, Coach James was a voracious reader who was constantly learning and looking for creative new ways to improve the Husky football program. Lifelong learning, he told me, was the single thing that helped him most in his career.*

Pete went on to write,

> *Throughout his exceptional career, Coach James helped every student who sought his assistance in an educational project—whether it was a quick interview with a reporter for the student newspaper or—in my case—a request for his active participation in a doctoral dissertation that involved multiple interviews over the course of several years.*

That is the kind of impact Coach James had on everyone he came in contact with. He demonstrated a love of learning and inspired others to become their best through hard work.

Coach James made sure we got a little time off to spend with our families on Sunday mornings. Some of us went to local churches and then we'd head back to UW to work the afternoon and evening.

The Perspective Change

Our first couple of years at the University of Washington were really tough. Coach James was slowly transforming the football program, but he was met with some resistance from the faculty, and a lot more from some of the established players. They were not happy about the sheer amount of work that Coach James required of them.

One of my players remembers me telling them, "Tape your ankles, lay your ears back, set your hair on fire, and go out there and cause a wreck."

The coaching staff had the job of working directly with the players. We not only dealt with football issues like effort, skill, and injuries, but also life issues like grades, family drama, girlfriend problems, and bad attitudes.

My life-changing "coach 'em up" moment came at this point.

Like I mentioned in the Introduction, this philosophy changed my whole perspective. I started seeing and treating the young men under my authority in a whole different way. Additionally, my goals changed from winning games to helping others win at life. Losses were no longer devastating. It was my goal every day to help my players be the best men they could be in the present and the future.

This perspective helped me understand that in order to gain excellence, the price is paid before the result. It's earned through patience, hard work, and overcoming adversity. In this process, I came to realize that neither my players nor I would become excellent if life was easy. We all needed to be pushed, and this football program was pushing me as a coach and as a person.

One of the things that naturally pushed me to work harder was being at a PAC-8 school. These universities were a major step up in their roles as educators and competitors, as well as in their reputations.

In 1915, four schools got together and created the Pacific Coast Conference. The University of Washington was one of them. The conference changed names and participants for the next 50 years. By 1968, there were eight teams competing in the Pacific-8 Conference or PAC-8. The universities involved were UW, Washington State, Oregon, Oregon State, UCLA, USC, Cal, and Stanford. Ten years later, Arizona and Arizona State were added, making the conference the Pacific-10 Conference or PAC-10. In 2011, two more teams were added, Utah and University of Colorado, changing the PAC-10 to the PAC-12 as it is presently. Only two universities have been in the conference consistently since its beginning in 1915, and the University of Washington is one of them.

The difference between coaching at Kent State and UW was like going from junior high school to high school. Everything was bigger, more intense and with a lot more people. At Kent State, we probably had 25,000-30,000 fans at the most, and Washington was at least double that number in the stands.

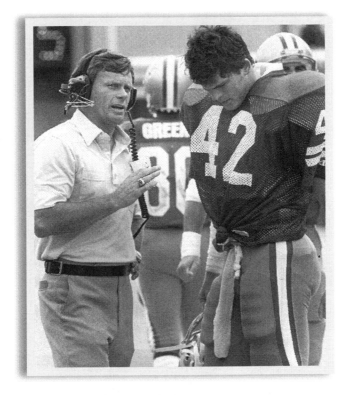

Coaching on the sidelines at UW

The PAC-8 conference was more competitive with a bigger stage, bigger audience, and a lot more pressure. Winning became more important than it had ever been.

The first year we were at Washington, 1975, we were 6-5. And unfortunately, the next year we were 5-6. Going into the third year, 1977, we were 11-11. That was not going to fly very long with the university, the boosters, or the fans. The beginning of the third year was even worse. We lost 3 out of the first 4 games. Coach James knew something needed to change drastically.

After losing the fourth game played, Coach called everybody into the team meeting room. Though we'd only lost by a field goal, we had still lost. He addressed everybody there in a very serious manner. He asked every player, coach, manager, and trainer to rethink their goals and determine how each person could help improve our football team in an individual way.

We all took it very seriously and wrote down things we felt we could do to improve it. We signed our papers and turned them in to him.

I wrote down specifics on technique drills to help the players improve the skills in their position. I also determined to be more attentive to them about learning what we needed to learn. The focus would be for the players to grasp the skill before they went out to the practice field. That way, they could practice it properly and be able to apply it to the game, where it really counted.

That mental exercise was not only a season-changing moment—it was a program-changing moment. The next week of practice was like World War III in intensity. Players were flying around, attitude was great, and everyone was putting in 100 percent.

Coaching at UW was an honor with Coach James
and excellent assistant coaches

That next Saturday we beat University of Oregon 54 to 0. During the rest of that season, we only added one more loss. At the end of it, we went on to win the PAC-8 Championship as well as play and beat Michigan in the Rose Bowl.

The key to our success? Teamwork. Everybody took responsibility and determined what they could do to give 100 percent. Nobody relied on anyone else to do their job or take their position. Everybody gave their all and when that happened, we won games.

Great leaders like Coach James know what to do and when to do it. He turned not only that year around, but the whole program as well. Great leaders and coaches know it's not about them, it's about how they influence and impact the people they're working with to become better. In this case, Coach James challenged everybody to step up. And they did—in a big way. This one challenge led us to bowl games for 10 straight years.

Coach James taught me that plans lead to success. Without plans, it's easy to get lost, lose focus, and miss the goal. He was a master planner and I was privileged to work under him. He planned every minute of every practice and planned the path to recruiting the best high school football players in the country, training them to work as a team, and win.

An article by Chris Landon of the *SB Nation* put it perfectly:

For James, the son of a blue-collar father, building the Huskies back up was a project that involved guts, grit and, most importantly, a blueprint. James did not aspire to install a quick fix and get rich off a few flashy seasons. To him, Washington wasn't some stopover on his career arc where his focus was to get some cheap wins and then move on. His focus was to build something that would endure and stand the test of time. To build something that the community would not only embrace, but would incorporate into their daily lives such that it would become part of their very identity. His blueprint was a process that consisted of the following components:

1. **Start with the character of his players he inherited:** *take boys and develop them into accountable and mature men. Make them leaders and examples for future players to follow.*

2. *Next,* **develop the identity of the team as a whole:** *the cornerstones would be toughness, fundamentals, defense, and attention to details.*

3. *Third,* **develop a personal network:** *take your branded product combined with your emerging credibility and parlay that into a network of high school coaches and parents who would want to send their young men into your care.*

That was it, in a nutshell. No extreme offensive philosophies. No promises to players of NFL riches. No fancy uniforms. No snazzy shoe companies. Just an enduring identity shepherded by a credible leader and a decent human being. It was a great formula, but it took years to implement.

Coach James didn't walk onto the campus of the University of Washington and start winning games. He developed a program, a blueprint, that brought in the best of the high school football stars and trained them to be excellent.

From 1-3 to the Rose Bowl

From the 1-3 start, the team, the university, and the entire state were overjoyed that we were going to the 1978 Rose Bowl in Pasadena, California. There was a new attitude for Husky fans. Before this winning streak, fans had not been known to support or encourage the players. We often dealt with our players being discouraged because of the boos at the games, or the discouragement they received because of their inability to play well and win games.

Our starting quarterback that third year was one of those guys. Warren Moon would come to Coach James, discouraged and disheartened because of all the talk from people that doubted him and his ability to lead the football team to victory. He was getting a lot of negative comments, not only because of his struggles on the football field, but also because of the color of his skin. He was a black quarterback in an era when most quarterbacks were white.

Derek Johnson recorded Warren Moon's words in *Husky Football in the Don James Era.*

> *At times it was really tough. I could hear the booing, but because of the track at Husky Stadium, I couldn't hear specific things that were being said. What bothered me the most was in knowing that my girlfriend and friends were in the stands and they were hearing some of the things that were being yelled at me. There were some times where they almost got into fistfights in their defense of me. It was real tough.*

> *I talked with Coach James many times about what was happening, regarding the pressure from fans and media. He told me that he was getting pressured by alumni to make a change at quarterback. But he told me that he felt I was the best at that position and he was going to continue to give me his full support . . . I owe a lot of my success to Don James.*

> *I guarantee you that going through that difficult experience helped make me a better quarterback later in my career. It also made me a stronger person. And going into the Rose Bowl in my senior season, we really felt like you could compete with anybody in the country, especially after the way we handled USC.*

USC had been a turning point in the attitude of both players and fans.

We were not expected to win, even though we had home team advantage and our boys were used to playing in the rain. USC had gone to the Rose Bowl eight out of the last 11 seasons. And they expected to go again.

We ended up beating them 28-10 and Moon, who led the fight, found the fans cheering him on for the first time. We were so close to going to the Rose Bowl. Nobody could stop talking about it, though Coach James forbade it in an edict to our team. The words "Rose Bowl" were forbidden. We still had one more game to win and UCLA needed to be knocked off by USC.

Both of those things happened.

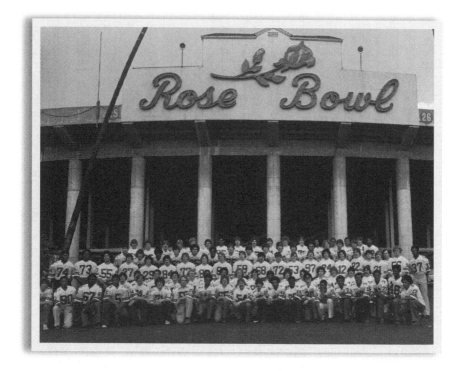

Rose Bowl winning team, 1978

The six weeks between our last game and the Rose Bowl were filled with practices, strategy meetings, nerves, excitement, and more practices. The anticipation we felt from the Husky fans, the university alumni, and the players was almost overwhelming.

Derek Johnson again clearly laid it out in his book. He summed up the feeling outside of the state of Washington.

The rest of the country didn't feel that way. Washington's opponent was to be the Michigan Wolverines, who were ranked third in the nation. When the odds-makers contrasted Michigan's 10-1 record with Washington's mark of 7-4, the Wolverines were made a staggering 14-point favorite. In betting terms, that meant Washington had no chance. The Michigan team itself demonstrated disdain for the Huskies, as Moon vividly recalled.

"When both teams were at Disneyland, they made it clear that they wanted to have very little to do with us," said Moon. "Rick Leach (UM's quarterback) refused to pose with me along with Mickey and Minnie Mouse, as was the tradition for the quarterbacks. I found out later that he had done that once or twice before, because he thought it distracted him from concentrating on the upcoming game . . . But especially at the time, it all served as extra motivation for us to prove ourselves."

We started out super strong in the first quarter when Moon got a touchdown. Then in the second quarter we got a field goal and another touchdown, all while shutting out Michigan. It wasn't until the third quarter and after another touchdown that Michigan finally snuck in a touchdown of their own. After one more field goal, we ended the third quarter 27-7. The fourth quarter was trickier for us. Michigan scored two more touchdowns but had a failed field goal. We were able to run the clock out and win 27-20.

This Rose Bowl win was a game changer and program changer for us. In the short term, it bolstered our spirits and ignited Husky fans. In the long term, this game marked the beginning of 10 years of dominating football and getting UW to bowl games. Personally, this game led to a transforming event in my life that changed both me and my family eternally.

We came back from the '78 Rose Bowl after beating Michigan. Everybody was excited, patting us on the back, giving us keys to the city, and telling us how great we were. And of course, we were lapping it up. It felt really good to be a team that Washington could be proud of instead of disappointing them time and time again. We were invited to fancy dinners, honored at ceremonies, and celebrated at every turn.

Virginia and the kids were ecstatic. They had loved the two weeks we were in Los Angeles having what seemed to be amazing vacations with all the other coaches' families. They had gotten a per diem and spent most of the days going to amusement parks, shopping, spending time at the beach, and seeing the sights. The win at the end was the icing on the cake for them. I also enjoyed seeing how much they loved it. It was a win-win. It felt like we had finally made it.

But a few days after getting home, Virginia took me aside and said to me, "You know Skip, when you stand before the Lord on Judgement Day, he's not going to ask you how many Rose Bowls you won, how many championships you won, how many players you sent to the NFL, or how many All-American players you've coached. What He *is* going to ask you, however, is what kind of a relationship you have had with Him and with me, your wife, and with your children, and what's been taught in the home." Well, that hit me like a 300-pound defensive end. It just flattened me. After hearing that, I knew nothing was ever going to be the same.

7

Seeds are Sown

Virginia had attended a Billy Graham crusade in Seattle in 1976, and she had come back completely different. I remember vividly, after she had returned, we were driving to a booster function—a big party put on by the boosters.

She didn't really want to go, and I said, "Well, Virginia, you're no fun anymore." I had seen this change in her, but I didn't understand the whole picture. I didn't understand the personal relationship with Jesus that had changed her perspective, her world view, and her heart. She wasn't impressed with all that stuff—the booster stuff and all the drinking that was going on. She had an eternal view now and wished with her whole heart that I could have the same.

I hadn't understood at the time because I thought we were doing what we needed to do to get to heaven. We had started attending church every Sunday after my confirmation class in Concordia my senior year. What else was there?

I soon realized that a commitment would need to be made—a commitment to follow God wholeheartedly. I couldn't just ask Him to bless my life and make me successful in everything that I did. I needed to follow Him and ask Him for His path and His vision for my life.

COACH 'EM UP

That realization took a few months. The question Virginia asked me after that first Rose Bowl win percolated in me for a while and I started to look at my life, my work, and my decisions a little differently. I started reading the Bible regularly and looked around for a Christian radio station that would "speak" to me. I soon found a guy named Chuck Swindoll on a Christian radio station and he became my companion and mentor every morning. Every day it sounded like he was talking directly to me.

I got a chance to meet and become friends with Chuck Swindoll a couple of years later. When we were in southern California for the 1980 Rose Bowl, I reached out to Chuck and offered tickets to him and his wife. He couldn't make it, but invited Virginia and I, our kids, and anyone else from the team who wanted to join us to visit his church. We went and heard him preach, and the next day went out to lunch with him and his wife. I found out that day that he is just as amazing in person as he came across on the radio.

Visiting Chuck Swindoll (second from right) with Joe Russell (left),
Wayne Wright (second from left), and Bruce Young (right)

That meeting started a friendship and mentorship that has lasted over 40 years. We stay in touch, texting or emailing occasionally. He sends me a signed copy of every new book he writes. He led trips that Virginia and I joined with Insight for Living. We went through the Greek islands, sailing a nice ship with about 150 people. On that trip we stopped at all the different stops where the Apostle Paul traveled. On the second trip, we did the Reformation tour through Germany and Switzerland. This was also full of history and we went to many churches. Chuck preached many sermons, and his most memorable sermon to me was given on the spot where Martin Luther defended his thesis against the church and said, "Here I stand, I can do no other." That was a highlight.

Besides reading the Bible and listening to Chuck, there was also a Christian player—a captain on the Rose Bowl team, Mike Rohrbach—who challenged my beliefs. Mike was an outstanding young man. He was a good football player, but he was also involved with the Fellowship of Christian Athletes (FCA). We would meet and talk, and he encouraged me as a coach. Mike's example of God's heart for others spoke to me and made a great impact.

Mike and I got to be pretty close. I coached him and he witnessed to me.

Mike remembers:

I chose to attend the University of Washington because I felt the Lord ask me to be a witness and shine brightly for Him. I spent the first day in the crew house asking all of the players if they were Christians. I would introduce myself and shake their hand and ask, "By any chance are you a Christian?" A lot of guys looked at me like I was crazy. But I finally found one guy, Mike Baldassin, who was excited when I asked. He was a Christian too and when I told him that I wanted to start an FCA group, he was all for it.

We made signs and put them up everywhere and at our first meeting it was just him and me. That didn't discourage us. We kept meeting and slowly our two-person group grew.

After our first year, Coach James came in as the new head coach. The first time I met Coach Skip, I thought that he didn't look much older than us. He was this handsome guy that looked like Johnny Miller, the golfer. I appreciated his spirit. He had a sparkle to him and I was excited to play and be coached by Coach Hall. I never told him this, but when I started seeing him wearing baby blue leisure suits, I thought, "That's kinda cool." I decided that I needed one too.

But in all seriousness, Coach Hall had a tremendous impact on me. I wasn't the best player on the team. I wasn't the biggest, strongest, or fastest, but he saw some good leadership skills in me. He labeled the special teams the RTK's. Rohrbach's Trained Killers. I still love that title.

Both Coach Hall and Coach James surrounded themselves with great people and empowered them to do great things.

Coach Hall did great things with a group of young guys, linebackers from all different walks of life, and brought us together and made us a unified cohesive group. He inspired us to consider being great.

I was a bold college student who loved Jesus and wanted to share that with everybody, including the coaches. I would give FCA Bibles to them and share with them about how important my relationship with Jesus was. Coach Hall was one of my most supportive coaches. He encouraged me to talk and share.

I didn't realize at the time what an impact I had on him. But he saw something in me spiritually. I in turn was encouraged and uplifted by him. He really did coach me up.

After Mike graduated, he became the state director of the FCA and today leads Run to Win—a ministry for reaching elementary students. He was a chaplain for the Husky football team for 16 years and is now chaplain of the Husky basketball team. He asked me to be the president of his board and so I was president of the FCA board for a number of years. What spoke to me the most about Mike was the way he conducted his life, more than anything. The way he lived his faith was more than just words. His relationship with Jesus impacted how he conducted himself in every area of life.

One thing that really impressed me was when Mike had a really bad injury his junior year. He messed up his ankle and tore the ligaments. Though he was in bad shape, his attitude never changed. He was still rah-rah Mike.

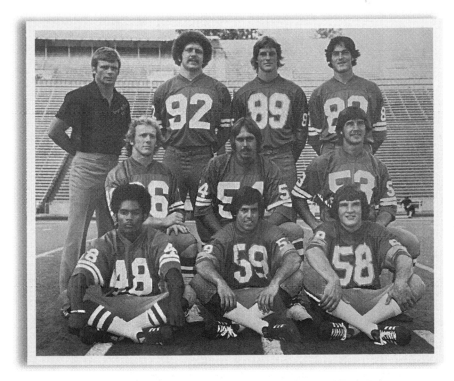

Me and the RTKs (Mike Rohrbach is in the middle, #54)

Dan Raley wrote an article about Mike in January 2021 for Husky Maven in *FanNation*. He wrote:

> *This determined player [Mike] and his dedicated fourth-down specialists were known as RTKs—Rohrbach's Trained Killers.*
>
> *Rohrbach and his crew were so adept at creating mayhem with punters and those trying to protect them that then-UW assistant coach Skip Hall slapped the RTK label on them. Among the special-teams leader's highlights:*
>
> *In 1975, Rohrbach scooped up a punt blocked by teammate Spider Gaines and returned it four yards for a touchdown in a 24-21 defeat to Stanford at Husky Stadium.*
>
> *In 1977, Rohrbach rushed in to block a third-quarter USC punt that led to a Joe Steele scoring run, ignited the UW's 28-10 victory and brought a Rose Bowl berth.*
>
> *"The USC play was bigger than the touchdown because Don James said it was the pivotal play of the game," he said.*
>
> *Mike led the first public prayer at a football game at Husky Stadium, kneeling with Stanford players in the end zone. A broadcaster was so confused by their actions he surmised that everyone was looking for a contact lens.*

A Spiritual 180

My official heart and life change came one day in May 1979, about four months after Virginia's life-changing question. I was on a recruiting trip in Portland, Oregon, and I was sitting in a hotel thinking, "Here I am, 34 years old, and I've attained the goal that I had—to coach in the Rose Bowl someday. So, what else is there?" Through the studying I'd been doing in the Bible and listening to Chuck, it dawned on me that there was something greater than all of this. I realized that I needed to surrender my life to Christ—which is exactly what I did that day in the hotel in Portland. I surrendered my life, my family, and my future to God.

I came home from the recruiting trip and told Virginia. She was so happy. Now we could be a team and work as a family together.

I began to understand God's plan for me as a husband and father. I slowly became more attentive to the needs of Virginia— more patient, which is always a hard one for a coach. I became a better father to the kids—more involved with them and what they were doing. I started becoming interested in things they were interested in—less self-focused.

As I look back now, I can see that the Lord saved me from myself and my own ego.

And I started to become a better coach. I was more interested in coaching the total person rather than just a winning football player. Obviously, we wanted to have a great football team and great players, but I also wanted to build great men for life and that concept carried over to the remaining positions I had as a coach. It was for this reason that I would get hired as a head coach years later at Boise State University to coach the Broncos on their blue turf.

After my spiritual transformation, small changes came to our children. No longer was church and God just a Mom thing, but Dad was different now too. We all started going to Sunday school before church and the kids got involved with church and FCA and attended FCA summer camps. Suzie even had a fear that I was going to give up coaching and become a preacher. I am thankful that the Lord never asked me to do that since I felt my gifts were focused on sports, coaching, recruiting, and team building.

Teenagers are a tough nut to crack. I mean, yeah, I coached hundreds of male teenage players, but one teenage daughter—she was over my head. But she was good, and she was very smart. She played several sports, but it was a shock to them at first when we changed direction in our faith. It just took our kids longer to make that personal commitment for themselves.

Suz was 13 and Chris was 8 during this transitional time. It changed the whole dynamics of the family when I became a Christian.

The way I think about my transformation to follow Jesus is this way: We were driving the boat, Virginia and I, and our two kids were waterskiing behind us. We're going one way and all of a sudden, we made a U-turn. The kids, of course, had to take a bigger, longer, wider path, and they both became believers.

I continued to have a close relationship with my mom

My mom had moved to Seattle in 1967 after my brother, Duane, was drafted into the U.S. Army, to be near my Uncle Everett. We would celebrate Christmas and Thanksgiving with her and Uncle Everett. We'd also have them over or go to one of their houses occasionally for dinner (during the off-season). They used to come to UW home football games and Suzie's and Chris' sporting events. The kids were really close to my mom and Uncle Everett and I was grateful for these relationships.

Duane was in the Pacific Northwest as well. In college he met a wonderful woman and had two boys. He was a good dad but he still struggled with the emotional aftereffects of the Vietnam War. He and his wife ended up getting divorced but remained friends and co-parents. Together they raised two good men, Jevon and Sam. Today Duane is in a veterans home for Alzheimer's patients.

Myself, Mom, and Duane, years later

Two of Virginia's siblings lived in Oak Harbor, Washington. The Carlsons and the Shermans each had four kids who were around Suzie's and Chris' ages. We got together with them regularly. The cousins were always happy to see each other.

When I became a Christian, my mom was confused. She didn't understand the commitment I had made. However, as she slowly saw how my family changed from our total surrender to God, she started to desire the same for herself. She began asking me questions about what I believed. During one of my visits to her house, she expressed an interest to know more. I asked if she wanted to pray and give her whole life to Christ. With tears in her eyes, she said yes. We got down on our knees in her living room and prayed together. She gave her heart to God. Thankfully a couple years later, I was able to lead Virgnia's father to the Lord.

We even saw changes in our neighborhood and with my fellow coaches. We started going to church every Sunday and the neighbors across the street would see us back out of the driveway and head up the hill to drive to church. They didn't know what we were doing. So finally one of the neighbors, Lana, asked Virginia, "Where are you guys going on Sunday mornings?"

"We're going to church." And of course, Virginia was really good about sharing her faith. She found out they were nonbelievers. She and Virginia would meet, and Virginia would tell her all the Biblical lessons she was learning. Wouldn't you know it, pretty soon, they started going to church and became Christians too. Steve and Lana Adams ended up owning the biggest Christian bookstore in the Seattle area.

Not only was my conversion a major event in our lives, but the other coaches found out I had accepted the Lord and started watching me very closely. When people make a commitment like that, other people watch to see how they're doing. One time, at the next season's Rose Bowl, we were at practice and one of our players was messing up. I said, "Brett, what the hell are you doing?"

Next thing I knew, Coach Chick Harris was excitedly yelling, "He swore! He swore!"

I knew everybody, coaches and players alike, were watching me closely. To my surprise, one by one, several of the coaches started becoming believers. Some had been Christians before, but the spiritual atmosphere among the coaches changed. Where we had been in a dark place spiritually, it became lighter and lighter. That was an amazing journey.

The UW James Gang

Coach James and his family were Christians and attended the same Lutheran church that Virginia and I did. One day Carol James called Virginia and asked her about being born again. Virginia said she almost dropped her cup of coffee. Virginia, who was a forthright, no-nonsense person, just shared her testimony. It really encouraged Carol.

When the coaches and families had committed their lives completely to God, that's when the real, deep growth started to come together for all of us and for our families and kids.

Wanting to meet with other strong Christians, Virginia and I decided to start a spiritual growth group. We wanted to get together with other couples to encourage each other and study the Bible together. We prayed about who to invite with the goal to keep it small. One of the couples that we invited was Norm and Bobbe Evans. Norm was an NFL player with the Houston Oilers, the Miami Dolphins, and finally the Seattle Seahawks. He and Bobbe were great encouragers with a solid faith. The group ended up having about six couples and we met faithfully every Thursday evening for over seven years at our home.

Football Chaplains of Solid Gold

Virginia and I had continued attending the Lutheran church that we had gone to since moving to Seattle. We were looking for a vibrant God-led gathering where we could learn and grow. We heard about an adult class from some friends of ours and how great it was, so Virginia and I decided to try it out. It was led by a couple named Chuck and Barb Snyder. Chuck and Barb attended Crossroads Baptist and the class was an adult Christian enrichment class called Joint Heirs. We enjoyed the class and the leaders so much that we started attending the church as well. It didn't matter to us what denomination it was, we loved it because it fed us. Jerry Mitchell, the pastor, was a great a teacher and preacher.

Chuck and I began a great relationship. We'd have breakfast together, do a study with other coaches that involved studying the Bible and praying together. Chuck and Barb eventually became chaplains of the football team and spoke into many football players' lives over the years. We held a Friday night chapel service at the hotel where they would give those in attendance a sound, applicable teaching from the Bible and pray for us. Chuck was also on the sidelines with us during the games—encouraging the players, even on the away games. They were tremendous encouragers and influencers.

Barb Snyder shares:

Chuck and I taught a Sunday school class at Crossroads. Skip and Virginia were attending another church and didn't feel like they were growing spiritually, so they began coming to our Sunday school class. They really enjoyed it and soon invited Don and Carol James to join them.

They all attended our class and we got to know them. They soon asked us if we would be interested in becoming the chaplains for the UW football team. Mike Lude met with us to see if we would be a good fit. He then invited us and we said yes. It was the first time they had a man and woman working together as chaplains.

As chaplains, we gave a chapel on Friday evenings where both Chuck and I would share about a certain subject. The meeting was only about 30-45 minutes. Most of the coaches and players attended even though it was not mandatory. In the beginning, there was very little response from the players. We found that with Don James in the room, the coaches and players took things really seriously. Finally at one chapel, Don James laughed out loud at a story I shared. Well, that was all it took to break the seriousness. After that, we found that the players started to engage and respond to our teaching. They also started coming to us afterward to shake Chuck's hand and give me a hug.

We also met with the coaches, players, and their wives or girlfriends individually and got to know them, pray for them, and love on them. Some of them were having personal problems and came to Chuck or me for advice, support, encouragement, and prayer. We both had many opportunities to share about the Lord with them and pray for both coaches and players. It was a wonderful time.

We found that half of our ministry was with the coaches. Chuck had a big heart for them and found ways to encourage them. He would pick up sweets and bring them to the late-night coaches' meetings. We would also invite them to our home and have dinner with them and their families. It was a friendship ministry.

I had a lot of opportunity to minister to the coaches' wives. I would meet with them, especially when they were struggling. I was even able to pray with some and lead them to the Lord. That was how it was with the students too. I would meet with the players' wives and girlfriends, really anyone who needed me.

Chuck met with the coaches to encourage them and have fun together. We would get together to study the Bible and pray. We also started playing pickleball together. Chuck and I became the pickleball champs among the coaches.

We had two chaplains prior to Chuck and Barb. These men were not providing the type of spiritual leadership that we desired. I knew things needed to change so I went to Coach James and said, "Coach, we have a problem here. We've got some guys for chaplains who aren't really good role models. I've got a couple that I think would be really, really good—Chuck and Barb Snyder." Coach James thought that was a great idea.

Not sure how to proceed, I asked, "But what will we do with these others?"

Coach James said, "I'll fire them." And he did.

We brought on Chuck and Barb Snyder, who worked as co-chaplains together. Chuck even traveled with us and did all the chapel services for players and coaches.

Chuck was such a great encourager. In the locker room before the game, the players and coaches would all take a knee and hold a hand. They'd get a minute of silence to pray in their own way and then Chuck ended the prayer. The same thing happened after the game; first thing we did was come in and take a knee, hold a hand, and observe a moment of silence and then Chuck closed the prayer time.

The players loved Chuck and Barb and the way they presented things—practical things that mattered, not preachy things. The team responded really well to Chuck and the spiritual principles he taught. He also had a great sense of humor.

It was unique to have a husband-and-wife team as football chaplains. I think the players really appreciated the unique outlook of having a woman speak into their lives.

Chuck and Barb were available to meet with the players or coaches who needed support or advice with their struggles or choices. They were always encouraging and were real parental figures to the young men who were away from home and family.

Chuck and Barb were the Husky football chaplains for six years. They traveled with us and poured their hearts and lives into the men in the football program. After six years, they really felt the Lord ask them to focus on ministering to married couples. Since most of the football players were single, they decided to give up their job as chaplains and dive headfirst into marriage ministry.

After having such wonderful chaplains, Coach James kept his eye open for another person who could be that spiritual guide to the players and coaches at UW. He soon found a great replacement in Mike Rohrbach.

◄ 8 ►

The Camelot Years

Our years at UW continued rolling along. We had a different perspective after our complete 180-degree conversion to Christ, but we were no less dedicated to the team God had given us to coach.

The 10 years when we went to bowl games every year, 1977-1986, I call our Camelot Years. They were filled with personal growth, family growth, and team growth. We worked hard and won big.

The coaches at the University of Washington during the Camelot years

The kids got to go to all the bowl games. We flew to Hawaii a couple times, the Rose Bowl three times, the Orange Bowl in Florida, and then the Sun Bowl in Texas, plus some other bowls in the Los Angeles area in southern California. During these trips, the kids got carte blanche plus a stipend every day, so they'd go to Disneyland, Disney World, and other fun activities. Chris was even a ball boy at the Orange Bowl.

In the off-season, after the bowl games, we began our recruiting schedule. We had a bit more time at home in the evenings, but also more trips around our assigned areas to meet the high schoolers we wanted to evaluate. I took Chris with me on some of the recruiting trips. He was always excited to join and was a real asset with his enthusiasm.

We were responsible for evaluating the players in our assigned areas and then bringing back film and evaluating that. We'd ask 10 tough questions in addition to things like height, weight, speed, film grades, and comments from others. We also talked with as many people as we could at the school. My recruiting area was from Seattle to Sacramento.

The key to recruiting was the evaluation process—that was our secret sauce.

Coach James ran recruiting like he had done at Kent State. He brought the recruits in for campus visits as well as traveling to visit players' homes.

We always held recruiting visits for the players and families at the James' home, and Carol and the coaches' wives prepared Sunday brunch. The wives were a big part of recruiting. They talked to the players and to the parents. We had anywhere from 40-80 people at these meals. We did it every weekend for a number of weeks during the recruiting period, from the end of November to early February.

It was a personal, family thing. A lot of players said when they had their official visit, they felt like it was a family. That was our goal.

Carol James was really proud of the unique culture she and Don cultivated in the football community at UW.

Don and I wanted our players to experience having a family while they were at university. So we got the coaches, their wives, and kids involved in making a family atmosphere and welcoming the players.

We invited every recruit and their parents to our home on Sunday morning for brunch, which was put on by the coaches' wives. It was a great way for them to find out a little bit about what they could expect once they joined the football program.

It was very unusual for high school recruits to be in the home of the head coach, but we wanted them to feel like family when they joined the James gang. We wanted them all to feel comfortable, and after the recruits left, I wrote every parent about their son and told them how much we appreciated their son. I wanted them to know that he was a person, not just a number to us. I would include our phone number and offer to answer any questions or concerns they had. We wanted them all, even the parents, to feel like we were family.

Both Don and I came from extremely close families. We started dating when we were 14 years old and were always very family oriented. We wanted to extend that feeling to others who hadn't grown up in a close family atmosphere.

Another way we cultivated family was by carefully choosing assistant coaches who were young, energetic men with good character. We were and still are a close-knit football family.

The James' home was on the east side. Carol had one big room decorated with Husky memorabilia and pictures of the James gang. The players were brought there to have a nice meal and visit with players and assistant coaches.

Recruiting From the Heart

Coach James taught us how to recruit. He devised the worksheet to evaluate high school football players that we used as we went out and recruited. But as far as personal communication, we couldn't have a script for that. We had to be the salespeople there. I always went after the mothers. I figured if I could win over the mother, I had a pretty good chance of getting her son to commit to University of Washington.

My personal philosophy on recruiting was to speak to the heart—not just speak football but also academics. Obviously football was important, but character development and family was very important too. Parents liked that, but it wasn't just talk. We lived it. They knew football could get their son an education, but they knew that turning him into a man was the bigger picture.

I was named one of the top recruiters on the West Coast at that time. It was my personal style of recruiting and being able to communicate with sincerity. I recruited a lot of really good players—some became All-Americans and first-round draft choices.

Back in those days, signing day was one particular day in February, and spring ball started around the first of April. One signing day in 1984, I drove to the Seattle airport and took a commercial flight to Portland, Oregon. I signed two players there, then I was picked up in a private plane by a friend, Lex Mitchell. We flew to the Tacoma area where I signed several more players. He then flew me over to Port Angeles where I caught a ferry to Bainbridge to sign two more high school football seniors. That day I traveled by land, air, and sea.

Even though signing day was past, we were out recruiting until late in May, recruiting for the next year. We'd prioritize talking to the coaches and getting recommendations on who they thought we should look at. After spring recruiting came the vacation. The coaching staff got three weeks off before football camp. We had to schedule it so there was still somebody at the office taking care of details and issues relating to players.

Sometimes in the recruiting process, it was really hard for a young player to make a decision. He'd have all these good schools recruiting him and didn't know how to choose.

Doug Martin and Ron Holmes were my two toughest recruiting projects because they were so highly sought after as high school stars. It was frustrating because I met with them and their families, and when I left their homes, it seemed that they were committed to UW. The next night, another coach from another school would be at their home and they'd get confused. I'd have to go back and re-recruit them. I found that I had to re-recruit the recruits until I got them signed. When they came to campus, I had to re-recruit them some more until they could stand on their own two feet with their decision. I tell leaders even now that you just might have to keep recruiting your work team members.

Doug Martin was actually kidnapped by another school the night before their letter of intent. It was a school in the California University system. They had kept Doug away from his home too long and his parents were concerned. When I called to talk to Doug the night before the letter of intent, his parents mentioned that they were worried because he hadn't come home when he told them he would. They informed me that the recruiter had taken him out to do some things and just never returned. They didn't lock him up somewhere or hide him in a cave or anything, but they had kept him busy—so busy that other schools couldn't talk to him.

The parents finally got a hold of the coach and said, "Hey, you need to bring Doug home." He didn't sign that next morning with

UW. He was still confused. The academic advisor for UW at the time, Gertrude Peoples, was in California in a recruiting role too. The two of us were working on him pretty hard and we had the parents on our side. They really liked Gertrude. She was a black woman and Doug was a black player. She was going to help him with his academics and they liked that. Gertrude and I went back to their house the next day. We were just talking, sitting in the living room—the mom, the dad, Doug, Gertrude, and myself. As we talked, Doug rocked in his chair back and forth. I'm sure he was in deep thought.

All of a sudden, the chair stopped rocking. It was so abrupt that we stopped talking and looked at Doug. He announced, "I've made up my mind. I'm going to Washington."

That was an electric moment. Doug didn't have much in his pocket when he came to UW but ended up signing as a first-round draft choice in the NFL. He was a really humble guy.

After his college career, as he was going to the Vikings, he said, "Coach, do you mind if I leave my car in the extra driveway at your house while I'm gone?" I told him I didn't mind. It turned out that it was a 450 SL Mercedes. All the neighbors thought we had struck it rich. He went on to have a great career.

Another recruit, Ron Holmes, lived on a military base outside of Tacoma. We had to have special permission to enter the military base.

At that time Abner Thomas was with me. Abner was my "ace in the hole." Both he and Gertrude were my winning tickets. When I really needed to put the clamps on somebody, I'd bring along one of those two, or both! Abner was military police and he was head of security at the airport.

When we got to the gate on our way to visit Ron and his family, Abner said, "Coachy," (he always called me Coachy) "you wait here." He got out of the car and went into the little station there. I could see him talking to the guards. He came back out and said, "Okay, we're all set."

I asked, "What did you tell those guys?"

Abner replied, "I said, if any cars with Oregon plates come up, don't let them in!" It was a brilliant move because Oregon was in hot pursuit of Ron, too. We ended up having a great time with Ron and his mom and sisters. He signed with us and became an All-American and a first-round draft pick, and played four years for the Buccaneers and four years for the Broncos.

Two other players who I personally coached, Mark Stewart and Tony Caldwell, became All-Americans. I was really proud of all of my recruits and players.

I loved coaching amazing young men

Jimmy Rogers was another amazing player. He had been heavily recruited by big schools like Notre Dame. I met with him and his family in Oregon. After some deliberation, Jimmy and his parents decided to accept the offer from the University of Washington. We were glad to welcome him into our Husky family.

Jimmy ended up being a tremendous safety and one of the hardest-hitting players I ever coached. In his fifth year, he was elected one of the team captains and we went to the Orange Bowl in Miami. We played hard and beat #2-ranked Oklahoma that year. Jimmy and I have stayed in touch throughout the years. I'm proud to say he was one of those who led the charge to fund the eight-foot statue of Don James that is now in front of the Huskies' stadium. He now has a podcast called *The Downtown Dawgs with Jimmy Rogers,* where he interviews and connects former and current UW players and coaches.

Jacque Robinson was another talented Husky player. Jacque was a tremendous player who ended up being the first freshman to win Player of the Game and the only player in the history of college football to win MVP of both the Orange Bowl and the Rose Bowl. He went on to play in the NFL for the Philadelphia Eagles, and in 2019 was inducted into the Rose Bowl Hall of Fame.

Another highly talented student was Antowaine Richardson. Antowaine was a star linebacker. After his football career, he started and sang in an a capella band and also became an artist. In fact, years later he created a drawing of Jesus for me.

Lynn Madsen was another player who is still making an impact. He played professionally for five years after graduating from the University of Washington. He encountered many personal trage-dies, but he credits Don James and our football program for helping him overcome them. He is now working to compile a video library about UW for former Husky players, coaches, and fans. It is called the Don James Video Museum.

Tacoma, Washington, was a productive area of recruiting for me. I ended up recruiting from that area for 12 years. One of the many keys to successful Tacoma recruitment came during the University of Washington campus visit and tours. Laurel Lundberg was our Husky hostess and she made sure the young men enjoyed their visit and wanted to return to attend the university. Many great players came from Tacoma, including Ray Horton and Ron Milus, who both became NFL assistant coaches.

Some University of Washington players I recruited from the Tacoma area

A lot of the moms thanked me for offering their sons a chance—a lot of single moms, especially, were very grateful. I knew the dynamic because my mom *was that single mom*. I had a special place in my heart for those types of families. I had great admiration for single moms who were working and raising their kids. I used my own story as I recruited and shared my heart sincerely.

Human Challenges

Even during the Camelot years at UW, not everything was sunshine and roses. We still were human and coached humans. There were always problems. During any one season, we had 100 males in our program—students between the ages of 18 and 22.

Years later I was speaking at a baccalaureate service in Idaho, and I asked a rhetorical question, "Who would like to take care of 100 males between the ages of 18-22 years old?" To my surprise, three graduating girls in the front row raised their hands. The audience and I laughed.

What else could we expect, dealing with that many young men? One time, I was in my office and I got a call. The person on the other end said, "Is this Coach Hall?" and I said, "Yes."

"Well, one of your players is down here at the bus depot with a knife."

I said, "Well don't let him stab anybody. I'm coming down." I had to go and get my player. This guy was a character. I don't know that he would have stabbed anybody, but a knife didn't look good to the people there.

As you can see, there were always situations with the players, including girlfriend problems and academic problems. I was the academic advisor on the football staff. I coordinated details with Gertrude Peoples, who was a landmark pillar for the UW program. She was the academic counselor for football, basketball, and other sports. She would tell me if somebody's grades or attendance weren't up to snuff.

There was one player I'd recruited from Texas. He was a really, really good player. During his first semester, he wasn't doing well at all with his grades. His name was Willis Ray Mackey. I called him in and said, "Willis Ray, I'm looking at your grades here and if they don't pick up, you're going to be in the oil business."

"Oil business?" he asked.

I said, "Yeah. You're going to be pumping gas at 7-Eleven!" And wouldn't you know, he picked up his performance. In fact, he scored a touchdown his freshman year against Texas, one of the other schools that had been recruiting him. He eventually became the superintendent of a school district in Texas. He really shaped up.

It wasn't all academics—sometimes it was conduct issues. Gertrude and I stayed on top of both conduct and academics. If we sensed something was going south, we were on it before Coach James knew. If he heard about what was going on, he'd come marching into my office and say, "Look at this!"

I'd say, "Yeah, Coach. We're on it."

We also dealt with players wanting to quit. Good players. I remember vividly one really good player I'd recruited from Seattle in the Bainbridge area. His name was David Rill. David was a solid person as well as a really good football player. During his freshman year he popped his head into my office.

He said, "Coach, can I see you?" When I assured him that he could, he came in and shut the door. He said, "I'm thinking about quitting."

My heart rate went up about 50 beats per minute because this guy was a superstar. I asked him what was going on and he told me about the workload, being discouraged, and all the personal things he was going through at that time. We talked it through and came up with a game plan to get him some help. Because of that, he decided to stay. He became a great player and helped us win the Orange Bowl.

Similar situations occurred with a lot of players. They would come in their freshman year and were no longer high school football stars. Their girlfriends and family were back in their hometowns. All of a sudden, as college freshmen, they were at the bottom of the totem pole. On top of that, they didn't understand what went into preparing for games and winning.

One of the things that shocks both freshmen football players and football fans is the ratio of practice to performance. In college football, the amount of time spent practicing is not double the amount spent performing. It's not even 10 times the amount. It is on average a ratio of 600:13 minutes. Ten hours of practice to 13 minutes of actual game time from snap to whistle.

This is important for everyone to keep in mind when planning for success. You will put in 100 times more effort in the planning and practicing than in the performance and execution. And that planning can't be pie-in-the-sky plans. In order to be successful and win in life, your practices need to be laid out, planned, and scheduled. Success never happens by accident.

Don James' practices were carefully scripted. Each practice consisted of individual segments, then group segments, and then team segments. Good coaches understand that they have to practice strategically in order to execute with excellence.

Football games are played on Saturday but are won Sunday-Friday.

Good leaders understand that too. They have to have tactical rigor. They have to be committed to winning and be very well organized.

The Indomitable Coach Don James

My office was an open door to the players and other coaches. In fact, for most of my UW coaching career, my office was in a wing overlooking Lake Washington. Coach James' office was in the corner. When I became assistant head coach, he moved me right next door to him. There was an article in *The Seattle Times* that talked about me and said I was "just a Skip down the Hall from Coach James." I thought that was pretty clever.

Coach James and I coaching together at the Rose Bowl

One of the major draws for new players joining us at UW was Coach Don James himself. One year, *Sports Illustrated* wrote an article about the top three head coaches in college football:

#1 Don James

#2 Don James

#3 Don James

He and our program had come a long way since we first set foot at the University of Washington in 1975. When he walked up to the stadium for the first time, the banner across the top of the Husky's stadium entrance said, "Welcome Coach Don Jones."

Coach James taught me so much for the 18 years I worked under him. The *Chicago Tribune's* Mitch Lawrence interviewed me in 1986, a year after Don led the Huskies to a conference championship, an Orange Bowl win, and being ranked #2 in the nation. The article was titled "He's the Best Coach in the United States."

"Don's not interested in personal acclaim," said Skip Hall, the assistant head coach who has worked with James since both were Colorado assistants in 1969.

"He's only interested in the team and what it attains. He's very much a team player, and everyone on the team has a role to play. Don is the chairman of the board. He makes sure everything is tied together. I've been with him 18 years, and he has followed through on that same philosophy wherever he has been. His favorite slogan is, 'Isn't it wonderful what can be accomplished when no one cares who gets the credit?'"

Yet despite or because of his humility, Coach James was constantly in the newspapers.

In 1985 *The Seattle Times* wrote an article called "Don James, above it all, keeps his distance and UW keeps winning." They summed up Coach James when they wrote:

Although he may be viewed as something of a miracle-worker after taking over the floundering University of Washington football program in 1975 and transforming it into a perennial national power, Don James is not godlike; he's god-fearing. He is not all-powerful; he admits to weaknesses. He is not and doesn't want to be perceived as anything but what he is: just a college football coach, perhaps the best in the country, but, still, just a coach.

"I'm not sure I have that (immaculate) image, I don't want that image," says the 52-year-old head coach of the Huskies. I think the more that's printed by the media, the more articles that say Don James doesn't drink, doesn't smoke, doesn't swear, all these things, I'm not sure how that looks in print.

"All those things aren't true. You should see me after I miss a golf shot.'

This doesn't make him less of a person. It makes him more like one of us. He's more human than fans or players imagine. Like the rest of us, he has anguished over career moves, even wondering whether he's cut out to be a coach. He has had anxiety over his retirement plans, about mortgage rates, traffic jams, and, of course, about Saturday's opponent.

"I don't want to be associated with failure," the coach says.

"Before the game, when we're finished with everything, I do sit down and worry. You can't think about anything else. There is self-doubt.

"You wonder sometimes how you can beat anybody. They look so good on film.

"But that feeling is private. It would be dangerous for me to let them (players and coaches) know this," he says. "I go before them with a pretty good attitude."

That is the James method. He doesn't let the light shine on the inside. He keeps his emotions under a tight mental grip. His image is welded in place. He's always in control, always organized, always prepared. He's stolid. He is portrayed as calculated, disciplined, urban, erudite and, above all, principled.

Don was also a humble coach. In the top left-hand corner of his game day plan that listed plays and calls, he always printed "Give credit. Take blame." This was just one of the many things that showed his humility.

He was truly a great man.

Husky Legends

Don James
and
Skip Hall

Don and me coaching side by side at UW

One of the other reasons for our success was the men that Don James brought to support him. Rick Huegli was one of those men. Rick was our strength and conditioning coach. He knew exactly what he was doing and was excellent at getting our players ready to fight hard on the field. He was one of the keys to our success.

Mike Lude Remembers

After 12 years at UW and 18 years coaching with Don James, I started to look around at other opportunities. One of the people who influenced me to do this was our athletic director at the time, Mike Lude. He was our AD at Kent State as well and had known me and Don for that long. He was the one who hired Don James at Kent State.

Mike Lude remembers hiring Don as well as another impactful coach.

I was the first full-time Athletic Director at Kent State. They had just had the riots that had rocked the nation and I was brought in to save a struggling athletic program. Soon after arriving, the head football coach resigned and I needed to bring in someone who could pull the students, faculty, and the community together.

I had six names on an index card in my shirt pocket and the top name was Don James. I had planned to call Don Sunday morning, but before I had a chance to call him, he called me.

He said, "Mike, I'd like to have an interview for that head coaching job at Kent State."

I was happy to tell him, "Interesting. Your name is on a list of six coaches I've got here." I didn't tell him he was at the top of the list because I didn't want him to get a big head. I went on, "I'll tell you what, you put a clean shirt in your briefcase and head to the airport. There will be tickets at Stapleton Airport in Denver, and you come out here tomorrow, Monday, and we'll do an interview."

After that, there was no question that I was going to hire him. The president liked him. I liked him. So I hired Don James.

Then Don put together a staff. Skip, being the graduate assistant at University of Colorado, was of course picked by Coach James to be brought along to Kent State.

Don asked, "What do you think about me hiring Skip?"

I said, "Well, I think that's a great idea. He would have been on my staff anyhow if I'd had a spot for him. He will be a sensational recruiter and a wonderful personality working with the community and with the alumni."

Skip has an infectious personality. He is a wonderful person and a strong Christian individual. He fit in perfectly.

When I used to interview people to join my program, if it was a man, I always wanted to interview his wife if he had one. If it was a woman, I wanted to interview her husband. Because to have a really good team, you have to have somebody like Virginia. She was just outstanding. Together, Skip and Virginia were an absolutely wonderful bonus to our first staff at Kent State.

After four years of Don transforming that football program at Kent State, Joe Kearney, the athletic director at the University of Washington and a good friend of mine, contacted me and said, "You've told me so many good things about Don James, I'd like to interview him."

And that was the end of that.

I gave another coaching great his first full-time assistant coaching job, Nick Saban.

Nick was a graduate assistant. He had gotten hurt Don's first year at Kent State. It was Nick's senior year and we made him a student assistant and then a graduate assistant. After Don headed to UW, the new head coach came to me and said, "I would like to have Nick Saban as a linebacker coach."

I said, "Okay, bring him into my office and we'll talk to him."

He brought him in and I said, "Nick, if you want to make coaching a career, you couldn't have a better opportunity than to be right out of college and get a full-time assistant's job in a Division I program."

Nick responded, "Mr. Lude, that's what I want to do. I want to be a coach."

I said, "Okay then we're going to put you in that position."

And that's how Nick Saban got his start.

Coaching Opportunities

I knew that Mike Lude was always looking out for me and for my career. A few years after we'd been at UW and I had my spiritual 180, I had an opportunity to apply for a head coaching position at another university. I was young—35 or 36 years old. After going through the process of applying and being evaluated, I became a finalist for the head coaching position at Oregon State. They let us know and wanted to schedule a visit to see the campus, meet the players, and meet with a panel of people from both the school and the community. I said, "That sounds good, on one condition."

They asked, "What's that?"

I replied, "That my wife comes with me because we're a team." They agreed.

I was really excited about this possible job. It would have made me one of the youngest head coaches in college football at that time. I also knew that I had a shoo-in because of my success at recruiting. I had recruited in Oregon and stolen a lot of good players out of that state. They were probably thinking if they could get me, they could keep the players in Oregon.

They got us down there for three days—Friday, Saturday, Sunday. While we were there, there was constant positive feedback from them, "You're the ones we want," and patting us on the back. Until the last day. On the last day, I met with a group of people. I was seated at the end of the table and there were people all around from the community and from the University and they each asked me a question. They would fire off a question. I would fire off the answer.

We were clicking and things were going really well until we got to the 15th question or so. I can still remember what that guy asked. He was kind of an old rough fellow. He said to me, "Coach Hall, what's the most important thing in your life, and in five years where do you want to be?"

Well, I knew exactly what he wanted to hear and a year earlier before becoming a believer, I probably would have said, "Football is the most important thing and in five years we're going to be in the Rose Bowl." They probably would have all got up and cheered and that would have done it. I would have gotten the job hands down.

But that's not what I said. What I was led to say was this, "The most important thing in my life is my faith. And in five years I'll be wherever God wants me to be."

And that was the truth.

Well, you could have heard a pin drop. It was dead silent and I could almost hear the wheels in these people's heads going around. "We've got a religious fanatic here!"

I didn't get the job.

I was told afterward it was because of that answer.

This illustrates the change that had happened in me because of my commitment to God. For the first time in my life, I knew who was Number One. God's Lordship in my life was the most important thing to me.

When jobs came up, like Oregon State and Boise State, Mike Lude really got behind me. He said, "You know, you're going to be a strong candidate for the head coaching position here at Washington someday. Don's not leaving yet, but it would be good for you to go out and get some head coaching experience before he does." That made sense to me. I also started to get an itchy trigger finger because I had been at UW for 12 years. I wanted to have my own program.

I give the pro scouts the credit for my next coaching opportunity. They always came through Washington, and we'd spend time with them and talk to them about our players. Then they would end up talking to me about how, if the job at Boise State ever opens up, I really needed to look into it because it was such a special place. So, the pro scouts had planted that seed in my mind.

When the head coaching job at Boise State University did open up, I made an inquiry and was asked to send in my resume and some recommendations. Both Don James and Mike Lude gave me recommendations that were off the charts. The next thing I knew, Boise State invited Virginia and me to visit their campus. I met with their selection committee, and we went through all the interviewing again.

Before we even left to go back home, they had offered me the job.

◄ 9 ►

Head Coach on the Blue Turf

I didn't accept the head coaching position at Boise State University right away. Suzie had received a partial volleyball scholarship and an academic scholarship to the University of Puget Sound. She was a senior there and settled in and established with her own life and studies. It was Chris we needed to talk to about this move.

Chris was in the middle of his sophomore year at Lake Washington High School. He played football, basketball, and golf. He was the starting quarterback in football and a good player on the basketball team. If we took the job in Boise, it would be the toughest on him. In fact, just the night before we came back to Seattle, he had scored the winning basket at his basketball game.

When we got home, we sat down with him and told him we had a chance to move and for me to become the head coach of an amazing football program. It was a big punch in the gut for him. But being the good young man that he was, he said, "You know, I gotta roll with it." He realized it was a great opportunity for me and trusted that it would be a great opportunity for him too. Chris got on board and helped us get ready to move between his schoolwork and games.

One of the hardest things we faced when leaving Washington was saying goodbye to the James gang—Coach James, Carol, their kids, my fellow assistant coaches and their families, and the players—we were a tight-knit family.

The James Gang remains a close-knit family

On the final day before we flew out, I went into Coach James' office. I didn't want to get too emotional, but I wanted to tell him it had been a great ride. I thanked him for what he had done for me and our family. I thanked him for the 18 years he had been a mentor and leader to me.

As we were talking, I noticed that he had a Bible open on his desk. That image gave me a real sense of peace. The UW program was being led by a man who was being led by God.

The last thing I asked him was if he had any advice for me. He replied, "Yah. Get an early lead and hang on."

When we arrived in Boise, we got connected with a great Realtor, Carole Gill. She not only found us the perfect house, but she also arranged for Chris and Virginia to meet football, basketball, and golf coaches from the different high schools around the valley. Her son attended Boise High and she arranged for Chris to meet the coaches there and some key players from the sports teams, including her son. It came as no surprise that Chris picked Boise High to attend. He was glad to know some students when he began school.

The Hall family in blue and orange

Once we moved into the new house, Chris joined the golf team where he helped them become semi-finalists his sophomore year and state champions his junior year and senior year. He also played football as starting quarterback and was on the basketball team. It's amazing how sports can really help kids transition. He made friends with his fellow teammates almost immediately, although we did have a $300 phone bill those first couple months because he had to call his buddies back in Seattle. We didn't mind.

I like to tell a tongue-in-cheek story about when we first arrived in Boise. Virginia and I were driving around town looking for a home. We pulled into a gas station and the gas attendant arrived to fill our tank. He looked at me and recognized me from the media articles about me. He said, "Coach Hall, we are really pleased to have you here." Then he looked over at Virginia and said, "Virginia!" She looked at him and said, "Bill!" They hugged and talked for a few minutes. I thought that it was real interesting that even though we were new to town, she had an acquaintance.

Soon after we drove off I asked her, "Who was that?" She told me that Bill was a friend from way back. I said, "That's really interesting. Here you are married to the head football coach of Boise State. You could have married Bill the gas station guy." She looked me straight in the eye and said, "Skip, don't be silly. If I had married him, he'd be the coach and you'd be pumping gas."

This made-up story speaks the truth about how much Virginia's love and support propelled me to do great things. In fact, I have never forgotten all of the people who have helped me along the way.

It was 1987 and I was 42 and the head coach of a well-known, well-respected university.

I had hired one graduate assistant from UW to come with me, Mike Snow, and I hired the assistant manager of the football program in Washington, Keith Brooks, to be our manager and director of operations at Boise State.

The year before I came, the first blue field was laid down. It was a big topic at that time. People didn't know what to think of the blue turf and some people didn't like it at all.

However, the media kept asking me, "What do you think of the blue field?"

I'd reply, "Well, it's the same length and the same width. It'll do."

I asked my wife what she thought, and she had a better answer: "It matches your eyes. You're going to look good standing on the sideline!"

On the blue turf as head coach of Boise State

The Important Issues

Coming to Boise State, I knew there were two important issues we needed to focus on with the players. One was the academic side. The other was character development. Players had been getting into trouble in both areas.

Gene Bleymaier was the Athletic Director. His big pitch to hire me was because of my academic results and high-integrity reputation. He told me, "We really need a Christian who can come in here with the right philosophy and do the kinds of things we'd like to do." Academics and character development—those were the two big areas they really wanted to emphasize. But of course, they wanted to win as well.

One of the things I am most pleased with is the legacy we left at Boise State. We recruited not only good players, but people of strong character—people who went on to become doctors, lawyers, and other community builders.

When I first got to Boise State, I took a look at the players' grades and over a third of the team was academically ineligible to play. I was afraid I'd made a serious mistake. We had to immediately make huge changes. We needed the emphasis not only on football, but academic integrity and behavior as well.

We put tremendous focus on going to class, doing homework, getting the best grades they possibly could, and tutoring. We had an amazing academic advisor named Fred Goode. Fred had been a star running back at Boise State. He grew up in inner-city Sacramento and had worked and played his way out of a struggling background. He graduated from BSU and became a teacher at Treasure Valley Community College. Fred was even voted teacher of the year by his students. We were lucky to have him. He was soft-spoken but powerful.

Fred and I got together to talk about the academic problem at BSU. Fred was excited. He had wanted to focus the players on academics for a while and had talked to the other sports coaches about it. He knew he had the necessary support now because he had the head football coach on his side. We discussed all the ways we could encourage and equip our student players to get them ready for graduation into the real world.

Fred remembers how we did it.

I met with the new head football coach about the dismal academic record of the BSU football team. I told him we have got to make changes. Well, Skip Hall was all for that. He agreed that if his players needed to be on the field, they had to be in the classroom as well. And from there, Skip and I started working together at all times.

Skip was the type of man who, once he said, "This is what we're doing," I didn't have to worry about him doing it. The other coaches had a harder time with the follow-through, but once they saw that we were serious, they buckled down and worked with us. They started making sure their players were attending their classes.

We really knuckled down and implemented study halls and tutoring help. We hired more tutors to guide the players. That academic emphasis was applied pronto. Fred's role as academic advisor increased, and he was able to bring in other people to help. The academic advising department grew and developed.

In fact, Fred had the vision to create an academic center where the student athletes could work and get help with their studies. Fred tells the story:

When I first started as the academic advisor, the student athletes had to meet in various places to study and get help. I ran all over campus, making sure they were in the right place with the right people. I started thinking and dreaming about a place big enough where they could meet—an academic center.

I asked Gene Bleymaier if that was possible. He told me if I could find a place where one could be built, he would consider it. After that meeting, I walked back to my office, which was in the pavilion. As I was walking up to the building, I started thinking about the overhangs on the pavilion. I didn't know what they were used for, so I walked into Dexter King's office, who was the pavilion coordinator at the time. I asked him what was in the overhangs. He told me they just used them for storage.

I asked him to come outside with me. I said, "If we were to build from here up, would that be a problem for you and the pavilion staff?"

He asked, "What are you talking about?" I told him I wanted to build an academic center for the student athletes. He got real quiet and then suddenly said, "Fred! Let's go talk to the architect!"

So Dexter called the architect as soon as he got back to the office and we were able to meet with him that same day. Dexter had vision. He was so excited, talking about the academic center and adding on to the pavilion offices. The next thing I knew, the architect offered to draw up some plans.

I knew that what we were imagining would cost quite a sum, so I decided not to talk to Gene about it for a while. Well, at a football game a short while later, I was talking to Ed Peterson, an Idaho inventor. I shared with him my vision for a place where the student athletes could study and get academic help. I knew some of the other BSU head honchos were talking to him about helping fund a Bronco stadium expansion, so I didn't want to get him involved in my project too.

Well, a short time later, I got a phone call from Ed. He was meeting with Gene Blaymeir and the alumni relations director and mentioned my vision to them. He told me that instead of the stadium expansion, he wanted to give me the money to build the academic center. He told me, "I'm an academic guy. I believe in what you're trying to do."

That is how the Ed Peterson Preco Learning Center on the Boise State University campus came to be.

Ed Peterson and Kathy Haumann, Bronco Athletic Association,
and the plans for the Preco Learning Center at BSU

Photo credit: Special Collections and Archives, Boise State University

With all the changes we implemented to encourage academic excellence, we got some resistance. Some of the players balked at the upgraded academic rules and requirements. I had our assistant coaches go check on them in class to make sure they were there. If they weren't in class, they stayed after practice and did a lot of stadium-running regardless of how hard the practice may have been. This emphasized the message of academic importance loud and clear. Seeing their position coaches in their classrooms was a pretty powerful message. I had been the academic liaison at Washington before I came to Boise State, so I knew what worked and what didn't.

Changing the Rules for Bronco Boosters

During the first couple of months in my new job, I learned what was going on in the culture of the football program. One of the things that needed to change immediately was the amount of freedom the boosters had with the football team. The school was allowing four or five boosters into the locker room with the players—before the game, at halftime, after the game, and on the sidelines *with* the players during the game. I knew that boosters were good and necessary for college football. They supported the program financially, and they were ambassadors who helped raise money, morale, and support for the team. However, they could be a distraction around our players. They could act like team owners, demanding access to and control over the team and games. I couldn't allow that to happen.

The first thing I did was remove top boosters from the locker room, which didn't make them happy. I didn't want them sitting amongst the players while I talked to our team before the game. So I had a conversation with Gene Bleymaier and I said, "We're not allowing boosters into the locker room. No exceptions." I told Gene I didn't mind if he wanted to give them sideline passes, but I didn't want them in the players' section. We ended up allowing them on either end of the sidelines and behind the team area. They couldn't come where the players and coaches were and couldn't interact with them.

One time we had a particularly bad game. I knew that on Monday the boosters would be ready and loaded with questions at the weekly luncheon. "What was that?" "How come this?" I decided to head them off at the pass. I got up and I said, "You know, I've had this terrific headache all weekend after the game. I went to the doctor and they took X-rays. When the X-rays came back, the doctor said, 'The X-rays of Hall's head reveal nothing.'" That kind of broke them up. Sometimes you have to do it with humor. I had found over the years that mixing humor and stories really helped get my point across—even coaching players.

Boosters are necessary for a good college football program, but they have a tendency to get themselves and the team in trouble. One time there was a really good recruit from California. I was talking to a couple of the boosters about him, and they said, "Let's get on a plane and go get him."

I slowed them down and said, "It doesn't quite work that way here, you know. We've got to follow NCAA rules in regard to recruiting." You don't just jump on an airplane and go get somebody. I knew that they were hungry in Boise for good football players. And I found that sometimes I had to set stricter boundaries to make sure they didn't do things that could harm the program and the team.

As head coach of Boise State, that was the one rule that I was going to make and keep:

Don't hurt the team. The team comes first.

That was true for players, coaches, and boosters. We needed to do things the right way.

Fortunately, we had a lot of booster support. They were anxious for success. They really wanted to develop something special. However, at my first booster luncheon, I announced, "Academic integrity and character development are more important than winning any football game and you can put that on my tombstone."

I'm quite sure that some of the boosters were looking for a tombstone that afternoon to put my name on. That's not what they wanted to hear. They wanted to hear, "I want to win!" Winning goes well beyond the scoreboard.

Years later, after I was done coaching, people would ask me, "What was it like, 30 years of college coaching?"

I would respond, "Well, for starters, you got 100 males at any one time between the ages of 18 and 22. Then you got a bunch of boosters that *act* like they're 18 to 22. And *then,* you get a group of media people where some have a football IQ of 18 to 22!"

My Assistant Coaches and Spiritual Leaders

It wasn't a hard transition to go from assistant coach to head coach. I'd had an amazing example as a head coach for 18 years in Don James. I also knew the kind of program I wanted to implement. I knew that the key thing is handpicking your staff. They need to be good and motivated because they become very important as you develop your program. I worked hard to make sure we hired the best staff we could, with the means that we had. The staff is really the number one priority, once you get the job. You want to make sure you get people in the right positions and that they can do what you need them to do to.

Boise State coaches, 1987

Boise State coaches, 1991

Dick Arbuckle was my primary offensive coordinator, initially. He had coached at Oregon State and had been a head coach at a smaller college over there. John Gough became the defensive coordinator, and he had a background at Cal Berkeley. Those two guys were the two initial coordinators and that held fast for about three years before I made a change. I ended up hiring a lot of new guys—young guys like Chuck Pagano, Jim Fleming, Jay Mills, Scott Pelluer, Jim Zorn, Mike Lopez Jr., Mike Snow, and Jeff Murphy. I found them to be real brush beaters for recruiting. All of them were on their first jobs and because of that, they were out there, and they were getting after it. I enjoyed their spirit and drive. I also found Ron Thomson, who had a solid reputation and brought him on as our strength and conditioning coach.

In fact, Jay Mills became a head coach at University of Minnesota, Morris, and then Charleston Southern University. After that he went into ministry and became a pastor. Now he has a weekly YouTube series called *Chalk Talks* where he does a video about lessons learned from athletics and life.

Seattle Seahawks great Jim Zorn coached quarterbacks and later went on to be an NFL head coach of the Washington Redskins.

Jim Fleming became the head football coach at University of Rhode Island.

Some of our position coaches were definitely new to the coaching arena. What they lacked in expertise they made up for in enthusiasm. During our first game of my first season, we were about ready to start the initial kickoff, and the team doctor came up to me and said, "We have to take Chuck Pagano into the locker room. His heart is racing too fast. We need to make sure he's okay."

Chuck remembers the story:

It was the first game day of the season and it was a big day. By the time we were getting ready, I had already downed about three pots of coffee and was raring to go. My heart started racing and wouldn't calm down. The doctor saw me and told Coach

Hall. It took a little longer for my heart to settle down but then I was back at it and ready for the game.

They ended up taking him in and settling him down a little bit. Thankfully, when he came back out, he was okay. That was Chuck Pagano's first game and first true coaching assignment. He'd been a graduate assistant before that, but I'd hired him as a full-time linebacker coach.

Chuck was a good hire and he developed quickly. He stayed for two years and then headed to East Carolina University. He met his wife, Tina, here in Boise. Chuck is one of the most respected coaches in the NFL.

Chuck continues:

Skip had a vision and a plan when he came in. He wanted our football team to take on a new identity and culture, a culture of positivity and building relationships. He wanted a culture of accountability that was done the right way—not belittling but building each other up. When some of the coaches weren't positive and uplifting with the players, he addressed it and made sure they knew that wasn't the way he wanted things done. He was great at holding us all accountable for doing things the right way.

He was also extremely organized and detail oriented. That was something I learned from him as well. He wanted no stones unturned. He made sure everything was covered and addressed.

Another encouraging thing happened the first game of my head coaching career. I was able to fly Coach Charlie out to Boise to thank him. A couple of the boosters picked him up and took him golfing and then he stayed with the team, ate meals with us, and was on the sidelines with me during the game. I was excited to see him, show him around, and bless him like he had blessed me. I was his only player who had gone on to coach at the top level.

Our relationship started in 1960 and years later we still talked two to three times every year. Whenever we would take the family back to Minnesota to visit family, I connected with him. He proved that coaching, in football and in life, is at the foundation of success. He was and still is my hero.

Encouraging Another Charlie

When I came to Boise State, another guy named Charlie was the video guy. He'd get up in the crane, the tower, or the cherry picker and film every practice for the players and coaches to later look at for critiquing. He did the same thing on game day. He was an invaluable part of the coaching and improvement process.

At the end of the first year I was head coach, I called Charlie into my office and said, "Charlie, I really appreciate the job you've done for us this year. I've got something here for you." I'd gotten him a nice blue sweater with the Boise State football logo and a white shirt to go with it. I handed it to him. As I stood smiling at him, his shocked face and open mouth told me nothing. I had expected a quick "Thank you" and a handshake. Instead, I got big crocodile tears welling up and running down his face. In alarm, I said, "Charlie, what's the matter? Is it the wrong size?"

He said, "No, Coach. I've been here 11 years, and nobody has ever told me I was doing a good job."

This reminded me of the necessity of valuing people; I had grown up under mentors who encouraged me. It was sad to be the first one who had encouraged this man. We need to reward people and tell them when they're doing a good job. It is such a simple thing to do, yet so profound.

Together We Win

Though we were emphasizing academics and behavior, we didn't slack on football technique. We won the first four out of five games and started to build momentum. In our second game of the season, we shut down Cal State Northridge from scoring completely. We had a few hard losses that first season but ended the season 6-5. It was a good start to my head coaching career.

Getting dunked after a football game win

I was always looking for ways to improve the football program. Because of this, I ended up shuffling the staff around and hired a guy by the name of Steve Buratto. Steve became a real asset and had a different perspective because he had been coaching in the Canadian Football League.

I knew that having spiritual leaders and mentors was another way to improve and solidify the team. We had two really good chaplains for our football program. They were older gentlemen who had both been pastors. They both attended First Baptist Church, in downtown Boise at the time, which is now True Hope Downtown

Boise, our current church. We found them because my son, Chris, got to be friends with Lydia Van Hoogen. Lydia's dad was Barry Van Hoogen, who was a former pastor, and as I got to know the family a little bit, I determined Barry was a good choice for chaplain.

He had a friend who had been a pastor, Armond Taylor. Between the two of them, they did a great job of working with the players and dealing with problems. We had chapel service the nights before the games and had prayer before and after each game. I made sure it was the last thing we did before we went on the field and the first thing we did when we came in. I'd tell them to "take a knee and grab a hand." We gave them a minute of silence to pray in their own way before the chaplain's prayer.

At BSU we instilled the importance of team. I talked about it regularly, and I had a slogan put above the locker room door. As we went out to the field every day, coaches and players alike would reach up and slap it as a commitment. The slogan said, "Together We Win." I'd often reference it, "TWW." We wanted them to know that this was a team deal. We were doing this thing together. The BSU players bought into that. They began to understand that what happened in their dorms, in their classrooms, and in Boise impacted the entire team. It wasn't just about what happened on the football field.

Another thing that I emphasized before every practice was the mentality of letting go of all distractions and focusing 100% on the next task. One of my most talented players, Erik Helgeson—a brilliant All-American—shares about what he learned.

> *Coach Hall put me in a position to excel. He surrounded me with not only incredible teammates, but great coaches that worked hard on developing us for not only success on the field and classroom, but for life beyond The Blue.*

> *Before every practice, Coach Hall would line us up at the goal line. He would remind us to Be Here Now. He asked us to*

let go of all our worries, stresses, and plans so that we could focus 100% on the practice and give it our all. I really took those words to heart, not only on the football field, but in the classroom, and then later at work. Throughout my life, this skill enabled me to excel at whatever I was focusing on.

When I left, 95 percent of the players were graduating. There was a huge difference in the academic integrity of the team and great results in terms of character development. Academic integrity and character development are what I consider our legacy. We won a lot of games—over 60 percent, including going to the national semi-finals—during my time at Boise State. However, the academic shifts and the character development are what I am most proud to have accomplished.

◄ 10 ►

Establishing Roots in Idaho

As the head coach at Boise State, I implemented a schedule during the football season that was similar to the successful program we had at UW. The one thing I changed was Sunday. I really felt like coaches should have an entire day with their families. So Sundays, we all had the day off to go to church and spend time with family. The coaches could grade the game film at home. A lot of people questioned me about this choice. They wondered if giving everyone an entire day off would work. I stuck to my guns about this choice. I felt that God would honor the decision.

On Monday, the entire coaching staff came in early for a staff meeting at 7:30. At that meeting, I talked about what to focus on during practice that particular day and went through any other loose ends, like players' injuries and academics. Then we broke up and the coaches had offensive and defensive meetings, studying the film of the opponent for that week and starting to put together a game plan. I also always made sure we had a scouting report that the graduate assistants put together.

We also had a team meeting on Mondays, in addition to the player meetings. At the team meeting, my coaches gave an oral scouting report—the positions, the players, their height and weight, etc.

I made my remarks and set the tone for the week. And then we'd go to practice for one and a half hours, followed by the position coaches coming back together to study more film after dinner. Everyone knocked off around 10 p.m. Sometimes I had to chase them out.

Both Tuesday and Wednesday mornings were more staff meetings before the coaches broke up into offense and defensive meetings. We hammered academics at every single meeting. You get what you emphasize, and I emphasized it a lot. In the afternoon, we had another position meeting followed by a team practice.

The midweek days were the longer two-hour practice days with full pads. Every play had been scripted by the coaches on paper ahead of time. We knew what we wanted to call, what defense we wanted to have. After every segment of the practice, a horn blew. If it was a 10-minute period, after 10 minutes, the horn would blow. Bang! You're into a new period. I made sure it was well organized and scripted and there was no room for error, though we still had to coach the players to get them to do what we wanted them to do. I wanted the coaches to coach the players and I coached the coaches—Don James style.

Those nights we still came back together as coaches and continued watching the opponent, evaluating. We ate dinner at the training table. Tuesdays the coaches ended about 10 p.m., though I headed out a bit earlier because of an early morning men's Bible study on Wednesday with David Roper. Coaches need balance.

Thursday mornings, we had a staff meeting where we finalized our weekly game plan. We made sure that offense, defense, and special teams were in the positions we wanted them. We also went over the injury report and the academic report again.

Thursday's practice was a no-pads practice, so it was more of a mental practice, making sure the players knew where to line up and what their responsibilities were for the upcoming Saturday game. We ran scripted plays, but there was no hitting or tackling at a typical Thursday practice.

Thursday nights after practices, we were done for the day. Coaches could actually go home for dinner on Thursday if they wanted to and sometimes coaches' families came in for dinner to eat with the coaches who stayed. I made sure that Thursday night was free. That's when Virginia and I did our couples' Bible study group in our home.

Fridays brought the weekly staff meeting in preparation for the game. If we were traveling, we would leave Friday after the meeting. So Fridays varied depending on whether we were home or away. The all-important Friday morning staff meeting was a complete review of everything for the upcoming game. And we had an itinerary to go over that each player would get a copy of for the weekend. Everything was there that they needed to know: the time to be at the field, pregame meals, and when to be on the bus.

For the first few years, during home games, we stayed in the Red Lion that is now called the Riverside Hotel in Boise. The last couple of years I was in Boise, we decided to let the players stay at home in their own beds because sometimes they had trouble sleeping in a different bed. But we still kept it structured, even when we were no longer doing hotel stays for home games. We still had all our game day meals together. We still had our player meetings on Friday nights followed by a team meeting when we all came together: players, coaches, and staff, such as key support personnel. At this meeting, I would speak to the team again and remind them of the game goals. It was meant to be motivational and get everyone fired up. After that meeting, there was chapel. It was voluntary, but a lot of the players and coaches attended.

The next morning we'd get up and prep for the game. The great thing about those days was the games started at 1:30 on Saturday afternoon. It was consistent. Night games were the worst because it forced us to change the schedule in every aspect. You had to sit all day waiting for the game. But for day games, we would get up and have a pregame meal four hours before kickoff. After that, most guys would head to the training room. They had their own little rituals for getting ready. Then everyone dressed and the team and assistant coaches went out for pre-game warm-ups and that was all scripted too. Everything was scripted. Everyone knew exactly where we were going to be every minute.

Everyone performs better if they know exactly what is expected.

Players have come back to me years later and told me, "Coach, that was so good for me to learn." They learned so much about structure and being on time. It helped them learn responsibilities that made a difference in the rest of their lives.

This schedule and routine was hard but so good for evaluating, critiquing, and improving every aspect of the football program. We were a well-oiled machine.

As the head coach of BSU, I posed for a calendar for charity

I had the privilege as head coach of Boise State University to have my own news segment on channel 7 and the radio. The Skip Hall Show ran for all six years. Mark Johnson would interview me once a week. We showed clips and talked about the previous game and the upcoming game. I did the same thing on the radio with Paul J. Schneider on KBOI. On the radio show I answered questions from people calling in. It was really fun to work with those two guys. They were personable and professional.

Years later I interviewed Mark Johnson and Paul J. Schneider for *Game Plan for Life* in the same rooms *The Skip Hall Show* was recorded while I was head coach

The Hall Family Team

On the personal side, I'm very proud of something that our family started. I got involved with a men's study and Virginia got involved with a women's study in addition to a couples' group we started that met at our house. Having a couple of community groups was helpful for Virginia to connect with other women. She was a football widow during the season, and I was glad to see her making friends and discipling other women. Virginia led a Bible study for the coaches' wives and mentored many of the younger ones.

Relationships were one of the most important aspects of our six years in Boise. When we left and went to Missouri and then Arizona, we maintained all those relationships here in Boise. They became lifelong friends.

Relationships are more important than accomplishments.

While we were in Boise, Suzie was still in Washington. She graduated from college and while looking for a job, I connected her with Jon Miller at Boise Cascade. She aced her interview and got hired to a sales position in Kent, Washington, where she sold office furniture. That experience ignited her desire to design furniture and later do interior design.

In the fall of 1987, Suzie called us, announcing that she was getting married. We were so excited. She had been dating Bill Baumgartner and we really liked him. She set the wedding for the following summer, and Virginia dove headfirst into wedding planning. Suzie got married in Washington and we flew up before the wedding to help with the arrangements. They got married at a Presbyterian church near the University of Washington campus. The reception was held at the new Don James Center in Husky Stadium. There were over 500 people at the beautiful wedding and reception.

One of the players from Boise, a teacher from Boise High, used to fish for salmon in Alaska during the summers. He told me, "I'm going to send out some salmon for the wedding." Unfortunately, it never came. The morning of the wedding arrived, and we were in a panic. There were a few other options for the meal entrée, but salmon was supposed to be one of them. So, to solve the issue, I went down to the dock in Seattle and bought some salmon right off the boat. Suzie had planned to have salmon, so we were going to have salmon.

Besides this small problem, the wedding went off without a hitch. Suzie was beautiful and so happy. Giving her away at the altar was very emotional for me. It was something I knew was coming from the moment she was born, but it still hit me that she was grown and starting a life of her own. I was so proud of her.

A couple years later, Suzie and Bill gave us our first grandchild, Cassidy. It was another moment that made me so proud and happy. Suzie proved to be a great mom. Soon after that, Bill was offered an opportunity to either move to Boise or the San Francisco area with Hewlett-Packard. We were so glad he chose Boise. It was a blessing to have both of our kids here and our granddaughter, Cassidy, who would quickly be joined by another, Jadyn.

Suzie ended up working in retail for several months until a position at a local office furniture dealership opened up. Though it was a good job, she felt like she could do a lot more on her own. She wanted to build something, and so she started her own company, Cornerstone Design, later called Cornerstone Collective. Step by step she grew it from a one-woman operation to an amazing company that designs the interior décor of hospitals, event centers, and major hotels—Marriotts, Hiltons, and other great brands. She has really excelled in business, winning multiple awards from the *Idaho Business Review*, including Woman of the Year twice and CEO of Influence.

Chris did extraordinarily well in Boise as well. He joined me in coaching at Boise State as a student assistant coach. He did really well and found out that he loved coaching. He graduated from Boise High and was recruited to play golf at the University of Washington. I was so proud. That was our school. He had grown up there and knew it as well as I did.

Chris coaching with me as a student assistant coach

Chris started at UW as a student assistant coach for football under Don James and then became a grad assistant. He was there five years. He coached on offense, specifically quarterbacks, and helped the offensive coordinator. Between both of us, we went to six Rose Bowls and Chris was on the national championship team staff. I couldn't have been prouder.

After graduating from UW, he went on to coach at North Texas University. He was the quarterback coach for North Texas for a few years and then he coached in Iowa at Morningside College. He was the offensive coordinator there. It was hard having him so far away, but he was pursuing his dream and Virginia and I supported him.

Chris and I at the Rose Bowl in 1992

One really hard family thing happened during this time. My mom was diagnosed with lung cancer. When we got the call, she was so strong and told me very clearly about her condition. We prayed together, but when I offered to bring her to Boise, she told me she wanted to stay in Seattle as long as possible. Well, she went downhill pretty quickly and when she couldn't take care of herself anymore, Virginia packed her up and moved her in with us. She stayed with us for about six months while Virginia cared for her full time. Unfortunately, pretty soon my mom needed so much care that Virginia couldn't do it all.

We made the hard decision to move her to a care facility. We checked out a few of them and settled on a really beautiful one with an excellent reputation that was close by our house. They took really good care of her at the end of her life. Virginia, Suzie, Chris (when he was in Boise), and I visited her often, spending as much time as possible with her. We all got to know the other residents and made good memories. She passed away soon after Christmas 1991. We celebrated with her and had a really amazing time together. Suzie played the piano and we all sang Christmas carols together. Four days later she was gone. My strength and support growing up had passed to the next life to be whole and healed with Jesus.

We celebrated with a memorial service for her. Uncle Everett sang a special song and a few of us shared memories of her, including one of her other brothers, Leroy, who was able to join us from Minnesota. It was a beautiful time that made me remember the importance of family.

Establishing the Family Football Culture at Boise State

Coaching is more than somebody out there with a whistle and a loud voice telling you what to do. Coaching is about developing and valuing a player or person using the "five E's":

➤ Encourage – When you point out the good in a person, you inspire them to build on those characteristics. When you focus on what they are doing right, it motivates them on the inside to work and try harder.

➤ Educate – Giving the reason for a change, command, or rule helps others know and understand the "whys" of life. If they can understand the importance of the whys, they will "buy in" and motivate themselves.

➤ Edify – To educate someone morally or spiritually shows that you care about them as a person. You are not just teaching them their job, you are instructing their character.

➤ Exhort – Inside motivation takes emotions, the will to change. Exhorting happens when a coach or leader makes an appeal that reaches others' emotions.

➤ Example – Nothing you can say will make an impact if you don't do what you are telling others to do. The most powerful lesson you can give is with your actions.

The blend of these five E's is what you really want to do as you're building a team, a family, or a group of people in the business world. When you encourage, educate, edify, exhort, and lead by example, you value people.

I carried along the tradition of creating a family atmosphere with my team by valuing each young man we recruited. We did the same thing we had done at Kent State and Washington. As the head coach, I'd invite recruits and their parents to our house and have a nice meal along with my assistant coaches. Virginia and the coaches' wives did all the preparation and served the food. Players experienced a homey atmosphere. We had a big open area downstairs with pictures all over the walls of football stuff and a pool table in the middle where we held the gatherings.

We recruited a lot of kids from California. When they came from LA or the Bay Area to see what Boise, Idaho, was really like, they would be shocked. To this day, I still get, "Coach, thank you for recruiting me and bringing me to Boise." A lot of them still live in the area and they've married, had families, and work there. I was proud we opened up a whole new world for them. They really loved Boise.

We were focusing on recruiting more than great football players but also those who had the academics and character to match. The guys we recruited from Idaho, the Seattle area, the Portland area, California, and Colorado all had these characteristics. We wanted to build that culture.

Louis Ray, who is now a pastor, and Winky White were high school teammates out of the Denver area. They had all the qualities we were looking for that would be foundational for this new Bronco culture.

Winky was an electric player. He had really quick hands, was extremely fast, and made an exceptional receiver and punt-return guy. People got pretty excited about him. Duane Halliday was the quarterback who was already at BSU, and we brought in Mike Virden, who eventually became a starter. After that we brought in a couple of younger guys at quarterback, Jeff Mladenich from the Seattle area and Travis Stewart from Meridian, Idaho. By far, my favorite part of coaching is finding and giving opportunities to amazing young men. I knew without a doubt lives were changing.

For five straight years, we had solid winning seasons. The most memorable game was against Nevada in 1990, my fourth year when we had great senior leadership, including Erik Helgeson, Terry Heffner, Scott Russell, and others. Tim Leonard wrote about this semifinal game in an article published in *The Mane Attraction*.

> *Confident about the outcome, both teams squared off at mid-field with a boastful talk session moments before the kickoff. No one in the stadium that afternoon could imagine the dramatic outcome that would occur four hours later.*

We didn't start off very strong in the first quarter. I had to replace my starting quarterback who had led the team well up to that game. I put in Duane Halliday, who immediately delivered a dazzling performance. He was able to give us a much-needed boost to end the second quarter only six points behind, even though we had delivered Nevada 14 points through an intercepted pass and a fumble.

We were able to take the lead in the third quarter with two touchdowns. Our defense was led by Scott Russell and Erik Helgeson.

Both our team and University of Nevada did really well in the fourth quarter and ended it tied 45-45. Our guys were exhausted. I took the time to lay out our plan and encourage the team, knowing we could win and go on to the National Championship in Georgia.

We went on to battle through triple overtime against Nevada. In the last overtime, we failed to catch a touchdown pass. It was a hard defeat, but I was so proud of our team. Halliday had come off the bench to throw 382 yards without interception in just over two quarters of game time, which gave him BSU's fourth-highest passing total at that time. Tim Leonard said it best when he said:

> *The game had emotionally sapped the players, the coaching staff, and the spectators. It has become one of the most memorable games in Bronco history.*

My next two years ended with a record of 7-4 and 5-6. That last year we had lost most of the strong recruits we had brought on initially and we had a really young team. We ended up having to start some freshmen in the defensive backfield and they struggled.

I was asked in an interview once how long it took me to get over a loss as a coach. I responded with these words:

"I'm not sure that you ever get over a loss. I see losses in this light: they are going to help us become a better football team. Through a loss, we can learn some things about ourselves, about our team, that are going to help make us a better team the next week. I guess if there's value in losing, it's that it should help us find out what we can do to become a better team."

As a leader, we've got to work through hardship and be the example on how to handle adversity, knowing that struggle and resistance will only make us stronger if we can face it with the right mindset.

The Importance of Balance as a Leader

One of the things I have learned in my years as a busy coach and later as a business manager and recruiter is the need for balance. This quality in a person's life is a sign of health and maturity. Balance looks like keeping perspective when everything seems to be crumbling, having fun times as well as work times, having a personal life and a professional life, getting exercise and sitting to enjoy a movie, and understanding that you can't do it all and need help sometimes.

It is especially important for leaders. A well-balanced leader is a good leader. Leaders are examples and are constantly watched. I was always surprised at the influence I had with other coaches and players, not just by what I said, but more by how I acted. When they saw me lose graciously, treat my family with love, care about them on a personal level, go to church on Sunday, and work hard, they knew they had a good example to follow.

While I was head coach at Boise State, I met two men that became great friends: Bob Rice and Dick Rant. Bob and Dick were my fishing, hunting, and boating buddies. I got into some sticky situations during our advenures. One time we were fishing in the Payette River and I was wearing waders. I was standing in the middle of the river working my fishing pole, and the current knocked me off balance. I fell sideways into the river and my waders filled with water like a hot air balloon fills with hot air. The swift current carried me downstream a short way while I was yelling for help. Thankfully, the guys were able to get to me and pull me to the shore.

Another time, I was walking along the banks of the South Fork of the Boise River on a narrow path and almost stepped on a huge rattlesnake. I had my foot literally lifted up and I saw diamonds in front of me and I knew that wasn't good. I backed off and backed up and the snake shifted into the rocks.

In another experience, we went on a powerboat up a river toward a dam and the motor conked out. We had to paddle and drift our way to a spot where I got out of the boat, went up on the hill to find signal for my cell phone, and called for help.

Those two guys harass me about all of those adventures. They were and still are great friends along with their wonderful wives, Penny and Paula, who cooked us many great meals, especially my favorite dinner, meatloaf. We had great times together and they helped keep me balanced, challenging me to have fun adventures and making sure I had a place and people to laugh with. This is especially mportant because a coach's work hours are greater than most other jobs require.

Another way I stayed balanced was by using humor. I found that life was so much better when I could laugh at myself when I messed up, during hard circumstances, when connecting with people in my life (I enjoyed giving people nicknames), and when sharing truths to willing hearts.

Finding some time to relax during the downtime

Golf outings also brought balance to my life. It was a time when I could put aside my work and stress and just enjoy the game. One particular golfing trip will always stick out to me. I had brought Jim Mora Sr. to do a coaches' clinic in Boise. Jim was a coach I had coached with at Colorado and UW and who went on to coach the New Orleans Saints.

After the clinic, Jim and his wife, Connie, and Virginia and I went to Sun Valley to spend a couple of days relaxing and playing golf. When we were there, Jim and I were standing in line to sign up to play golf. Jim said, "Hey Skip, look who's next to you."

Well, I turned and standing right next to me was Clint Eastwood. That made my day. I introduced Jim and myself. We started chatting and ended up telling Clint that we were coaches. We quickly found out that Clint loved football and so we talked football for a bit. When we were done, I asked him if he would play along with me on something. He agreed and so Jim and I walked on each side of Clint out of the building to Connie and Virginia, who were sitting on the deck. Clint was a tall thin guy, about 6'6". We walked up to our wives, who didn't notice us until I addressed them. "Virginia, Connie, we'd like you to meet our new friend, Clint . . . Clint . . . Oh yeah, Clint Eastwood." Well, they looked up—way up, with their mouths hanging open. It was really hilarious. We had a good laugh about it for the rest of the day.

Balance became easier for me after giving my heart to Christ. I gained an understanding about what was essential. I comprehended that salvation, relationships, and people were what count, both during my time on earth and afterward. People are more important than things. As one of my mentors, Chuck Swindoll, asked, "Have you ever seen a hearse with a U-Haul behind it?" You can't take things with you into heaven.

Balance is about keeping perspective. It's about asking yourself what is really important. It's about understanding that what you are going through won't last forever and it's about keeping a heavenly perspective.

Experiencing Winds of Change

College football fans can be quite fickle sometimes. After winning a pretty significant game one fall, I was driving and noticed a large billboard that said, "Skip Hall for President." It made me chuckle. Well, two weeks later after we had lost a game, I walked out my front door to find a *For Sale* sign that some disgruntled fan had put on my front lawn. That is a common atmosphere around college football programs. If you were winning, they loved you but not so much if you were losing.

Unfortunately, in all six years, we could never beat the University of Idaho. They were our biggest rival, splitting the state like a football civil war. In the last defeat, I knew that my time as coach of this amazing football program was coming to an end. I had prayed about it all week, asking the Lord to show me the way. He was closing a door and though there wasn't an open door immediately, I had peace knowing that He knew our future.

I didn't know what the future held, but I knew Who held the future.

I called a meeting with the athletic director and the president, and they said, "What do you want to do?"

I said, "It's pretty clear to me that we need a change. The program needs a change. I need a change." We decided that's what we would do, and I would stay on for a few months until I got relocated.

I scheduled a televised press conference in Boise to make the announcement. I thanked everybody, the boosters, the coaches, the players, and the people who had been behind us. We received an outpouring of support and got hundreds of letters. I was deeply impacted by the encouragement we received at that time.

One other thing that had always been important to me was to help our assistant coaches get new jobs. It's not just the head coach that exits, it's also all the assistants and their families who have to transition to new locations and new jobs. After resigning, I worked hard to get our assistant coaches new assignments. All of them landed on their feet, and so I was able to take a deep breath. My guys were going to be okay.

Soon after putting the word out that I was looking for a new football gig, I interviewed for another head coaching position in Louisiana at Nichols State. They flew me down and I went through the interview. Nichols is Cajun country and though they did a good job of hiding most of the interesting Cajun traditions from me, it was still quite an experience. Trying to get a feel for the place, I had asked them what they did for recreation. "Hunt gators." And they warned me, "You gotta be careful because there are a lot of water moccasins out there."

The meeting at the university went really well and after I flew home, the university's president called. He said, "We want you and your wife to fly down here." I couldn't bring myself to do it because it had been a culture shock for me, and I knew that Virginia would not appreciate the wildlife or some of the stranger cultural aspects of Louisiana. I didn't have the heart to fly back down there with Virginia and tell them no. I just said, "I don't feel like this is the right fit." And so we passed.

Not too soon after, my coaching buddy of 14 years, Bob Stull, called. He was the head coach at the University of Missouri. He said, "It's time to go to work."

I said, "Okay. What do you have in mind?"

"I want you to be my defensive coordinator."

Bob remembers:

My relationship with Skip started when we were both hired by Don James at Kent State. We even split a salary. We became good friends hanging out at the 11th Frame, sharing recruiting stories, and getting into crazy situations as 20-year-olds. But over the years that we coached together, we both matured as men and as coaches.

I came to admire Skip. Over the years he had proved himself to be, not only an excellent recruiter, but also an excellent coach. He cared about his players, personally and professionally. He also knew how to get the best out of them, motivating them in the way that worked best for them individually. He had a way of talking and instructing that was clear, direct, and yet encouraging. He was just a really good coach.

And so, after barely any time off at all, it was back to coaching for us. And we were excited to be going to the Big 8. We really enjoyed the heritage of those types of universities. The alumni support and the traditions were easy for us because they were similar to the University of Washington and the PAC-12. In some ways, it felt like going home. It was back to the big time.

◄ 11 ►

On to Mizzou

Coach James had developed a tremendous coaching tree. He had "birthed" great coaches like Nick Saban, Jim Mora Sr., Ray Dorr, Bob Stull, Keith Gilbertson, Jim Heacock, Bob Wagner, Jeff Woodruff, Matt Simon, Dom Capers, and Jim Mora Jr. In turn these and other assistant coaches to Don James have gone on to create other great coaches. Andy Reid, Kirby Smart, Jimbo Fisher, Ed Orgeron, and Dan Mullen all came from the Don James coaching tree. In fact, nobody can calculate the impact he had on the college football coaching culture in the U.S., but it was huge.

Don James was also a major player in changing my and my family's lives. He was an incredible boss, coach, and friend. At the University of Washington, he was so beloved that they called him the "Dawgfather." Coach James had taken the UW football program to a level they had only dreamed about. He was so beloved that they had built a booster center and dedicated it to him, calling it the Don James Center. And then in 2020, the university unveiled an eight-and-a-half-foot statue of Don James. He was a legend. So in 1993, it was very upsetting to me to hear about the charges that the PAC-10 brought against the University of Washington and its football program.

Carol James was beloved as well. She was the heart behind the program, making each and every recruit feel like they were joining a family. If Don was called the "Dawgfather" then Carol was certainly the "Dawgmother."

Soon after moving to Missouri, my son, Chris, called me one morning. He said, "Coach James is going to resign."

I responded, "Wow, that's unbelievable." I really couldn't believe it. I hung up and I called Coach James directly. I asked him, "What's happening?"

I will never forget his reply. He simply said, "I'm history." He explained that he was retiring because of the over-the-top penalties levied at his football program. He was protesting the penalties that were assessed by the conference, UW's own conference. For some ridiculous reason, they wanted a *two-year* ban on postseason play, though the compliance committee only recommended one, and on top of that, their football scholarships were cut, television revenue was reduced, four boosters were ordered to disassociate, and three players lost their eligibility to play. He told me he would have been okay with a one-year ban, but two years was too much, and the conference didn't even let UW appeal—though the next year they added a rule in the books that said that the offending school has a right to appeal.

Coach James told the UW president, and the athletic director, "Look, I can live with one year, but two years is completely out of line. We didn't have anything to do with the infractions!"

Coach James figured that the other schools in the conference were jealous because we'd been to so many Rose Bowls. They voted for a two-year penalty. No bowl games. No post-season play.

If Coach James said something, he was going to do it. He said, "I'm history," and he walked away.

Many penalties were assessed to UW and they were the most severe that the PAC-10 had ever handed out against a member school. The penalties were similar in severity to repeat offender schools and the University of Washington was not one. This was the very first time any sanctions had been brought against the school under Don James. If fact, Coach James prided himself on running a clean program. He had no idea those things were going on. Chris was there as a student coach at that time, and he confirmed that none of the coaches had any idea.

The major issues came from the boosters. They thought they were helping the program, but they were what brought it down. They were paying players for employment that wasn't an official job—which is illegal. NCAA says you can't pay players unless they have a legitimate job.

Coach James was hurt. He knew he had turned the University into a football powerhouse, and he had poured his heart and soul into that program for over 18 years. He felt like the president and the new athletic director didn't fight for him. They let the other schools make the determination. I think the president was a bit jealous because the football program had become a giant.

One thing Coach James wanted to do was protect his assistants. He was glad when the university made Jim Lambright head coach because that meant that all the assistants would stay too. That was a relief for Coach James. Jim had been a Husky player and coach for 24 years starting in 1969 and had worked with Coach James for the entire time that Coach James was at Washington. Chris was still there for two years when Jim Lambright was the head coach and then he got a new coaching position elsewhere.

It was sad knowing that Coach James wouldn't be at UW anymore, but I had a new team to coach and I needed to focus on them.

The Move to Columbia

We moved to Columbia, Missouri, in 1993. We bought a new house and Virginia settled in while I dove into coaching. Being a part of a university in the Big 8 was amazing. It felt like we were back in the big time again playing Nebraska, Texas, and Oklahoma. I was pleased to be coaching again with Bob Stull.

This was the first official move without any children. It was incredibly hard on us, realizing we were moving away from Suzie and Chris. Suzie and her husband had given us our first grandchild, Cassidy, while I was head coach in Boise. Chris and Suzie had even taught her all the football signals. Chris would say, "Holding," and she'd give the signal. "Delay of game," and she'd give the signal. She had a whole show. She was a joy in our lives.

Chris was attending UW at the time, but still considered Boise home. Until we moved, he would fly back to Boise for summers and holidays. We realized he would need to grow his own roots now. Where that would be, we didn't know.

Once we got to Missouri, we called Suzie and Cassidy often. Chris was a little harder to get on the phone because of his classes and coaching schedule, but we connected as often as possible. They flew out for some home games in Columbia and would make their visits as long as possible.

God knew we were missing our kids, and he provided another "son" who I could disciple and "coach up." Upon arriving in Missouri, I inquired about our graduate assistants. I was told there had been two, but both had gotten full-time jobs and their spots needed to be filled. I put out the word and started looking at applications. Among the eight or so that I chose to interview was a young man by the name of Jeff Montgomery. He had been on the football team and had graduated from Mizzou the year before.

Jeff remembers the very first time he met me:

My soon-to-be wife and I drove to Columbia for the interview with Coach Hall, the new defensive coordinator at Mizzou. I went into the building for the interview and Lisa stayed in the car.

When Coach Hall called me, he was professional on the phone, and we set up the interview. I knew he had been the head coach at Boise State. I had prepared a bit, jotting down notes that I wanted to share—things I had done and wanted to do.

Well, I never even opened those notes. Talking to Coach Hall was like talking to an old friend. We connected right away. He put me at such ease that we just talked and shared our hearts with one another. During the conversation, I told him that I live my life with faith, family, and friends. I don't know if I believed that completely at the time, but I said it because I thought it was what other people wanted to hear.

Well, Coach Hall got quiet after I said that and then asked me, "Do you? Can you tell me about that?" So I started talking about my faith, my family, and my friends and how important each one was to me in my life. I told him about the beautiful blonde I had just asked to be my wife. He wanted to know more about her and I mentioned that she was sitting out in the car, reading a magazine.

By this time in the interview, it had been two and a half hours. He made me go get her and she joined us for the rest of the interview.

By the time I left, he had expressed his desire to have me on his team. He mentioned that he had a couple of other people he wanted to talk to, but it wouldn't take long.

The very next day I got a phone call from him. I was his official defensive graduate assistant.

I had a few more interviews for potential graduate assistants but Jeff stood out head and shoulders above the rest. He was so excited when I called him and told him he was the man for the job.

After that, God continued to knit our hearts, connecting with love and laughter. He affectionately became the football program's fall boy. He was blamed for any fault that the coaching staff (mostly the defense) had and admitted to it with a heart full of humility, even though we all knew that most things were not his fault.

Jeff got two nicknames right off the bat. We started calling him "Monty" because his last name was way too long. His other nickname was "The Gov." He received this one because he was always shaking hands with people at the basketball games and around campus like he was campaigning, though in truth, he just knew everybody and was well liked in return.

I encouraged him to attend church and we had deep conversations about what God was doing in our lives. At times, Virginia and I had Jeff and Lisa over for dinner. We enjoyed getting to know them as a couple, and we were excited to be there for them as they planned their wedding and started their life together.

Jeff was always very grateful for the way I included him in my life, on the field and off, but I truly enjoyed being with him and appreciated what he brought to my life.

Jeff said that one of the biggest lessons he learned from me was about how to act during adversity:

> The first year I was a graduate assistant, we had more losses than wins. In fact, after the first year, our head coach got reassigned. I watched Coach Skip roll through that year. It was tough on all of us.
>
> One game at the end of the abysmal season, we were playing our archrival, the University of Kansas. We had lost the final game and all the coaches were sitting in the locker room. Some of them knew they were getting fired and were tearing up their shirts and were really upset. They left and Skip and I were just sitting there. I made the comment, "Well, I better go love my family."
>
> Skip grabbed me by my shirt collar and as intense as he had ever been, he said, "Monty, I'm going to tell you one thing that

I have learned. Every day in this profession, when you walk out that door, there is always going to be somebody—your wife, kids, parents, someone—that is waiting on you because they love you and support you. They do not care about what just happened out on the field. They love you for you."

I will not ever forget that. Years later I was watching Bill Cowher with the Pittsburgh Steelers. They had just lost a Super Bowl, and he was walking off the field with tears in his eyes and his little daughter came up to him and just reached up her arms. He gave her the biggest hug and it was like, "Boom." There it is. That is exactly what Coach Skip was talking about all those years ago.

In my new position, I dove back into recruiting. Mizzou was a good university with a good reputation. They had experienced some hard years getting to football championships but had a record of being a winning school, which helped with recruiting. I continued with my signature style of recruiting—reaching the heart of the student athlete and connecting with his family. I was able to bring in some really good players who helped get the University of Missouri Tigers back to bowl games.

Five of the players I recruited were Brock Olivo, who played in the NFL for four years; Corby Jones, who played for the Canadian Football League; Devin West, a running back who went on to play professionally, and Mike Morris and Todd Neimeyer, two prominent offensive linemen who also went on the play professionally. These five young men became tremendous assets to the Mizzou football program and worked together to lead the Tigers to two consecutive bowl games after a 13-year bowl game drought.

While I was at Mizzou, the Tigers' leading tacklers were Darryl Major and Travis McDonald. As their coach, I liked to call them "D. Maj" and "T. Mac". They were great young men and we have stayed in touch for decades. I love these guys as well as all the players I recruited and coached.

Travis McDonald was a junior when I joined the Mizzou coaching staff. He shares about his transition as a position player under me.

When Coach Hall first arrived, I was kind of standoffish. We had gone through a couple of different changes and he was my third position coach. In the beginning, I stood back to see what kind of coach he would be.

I quickly found out that not only was he very knowledgeable with 25 years of coaching experience behind him, but he showed me that he genuinely cared about me. Because of that, I wanted to become the best player that I could be.

It really is true that no one will care how much you know until they know how much you care.

Years later when I became a coach myself, I took that philosophy to heart. I make sure that my players know that I genuinely care about them—on and off the field. That is how I can make the biggest impact in the lives of my young men.

Moving Into Prime Time

When we first moved to Missouri and were working on expanding our social circle, we attended a get-together at somebody's house. They asked me what my interests were and men's ministry came up. One lady said, "You sound just like Larry Glabe."

I asked, "Who's Larry Glabe?" She informed me that he was with The Navigators. I had heard of The Navigators in Colorado and their ministry to college students, but I didn't know they had a reach into Missouri. I was interested.

I got Larry's number from the lady and called him the following day. "Larry, this is Skip Hall, the new defensive coordinator at Mizzou." There was a long silence because he thought somebody was spoofing him. I told him why I was calling, and we decided to get together for lunch. We met and connected with a shared passion for reaching businessmen and connecting them through the study of God's word. It was a passion with a purpose.

We ended up meeting several times and eventually invited several other businessmen to join us—Jack Needy, who owned all the Burger Kings in the area; Bill Moore, a pastor; physicians Dr. David Parsons and Dr. Jim Coy; and others. We launched a Wednesday morning men's study called Prime Time. It was early in the morning, 6:30 to 7:30, so the men could get to work.

Larry remembers the powerful meetings, growth, and breakthroughs that we had during those years and beyond:

I never had a division 1 college football coach call me before, so when Coach said, "This is Coach Skip Hall from the University of Missouri," I was stunned. He went on to explain, "My profession is coaching football, but my passion is to follow Christ and encourage others to do the same." He used his platform to embrace his passion. I was pretty excited and expressed interest in meeting with him.

We met the next day and I shared about how God had called me to reach businessmen with the gospel of Christ. I shared that at the end of 1989, God had challenged me with a quote by Henry David Thoreau. "The mass of men lead lives of quiet desperation." God had awakened in me a longing to show men the relationship with God that could lead them out of their quiet desperation. In addition, if we could reach a man, we could in turn impact his family.

The more I shared, the more excited Skip became. He shared that he felt like a spiritual jockey wherever he goes. He is always looking for a horse to ride. We connected about our mutual desire to be spiritual coaches to men. He had a fun twinkle in his eye as we shared. I asked at the end of our get-together, "Coach, where do we go from here?"

He answered, "Well, we saddle up." I felt like I had just been introduced to my best friend.

We began to meet, pray and brainstorm. Almost daily around noon I would get a phone call and hear this enthusiastic greeting, "Coach Glabe, this is Skipper T, mobile one to base. What is going on?" I would always laugh, but that was his way of wanting to connect. Sometimes the phone call would be 10 minutes and sometimes it would be 30. This is how we built our friendship—time spent together and two-way communication. During the times we connected, we shared with each other what God had laid on our hearts.

In the early spring of 1992, Coach and I were having lunch at the Dairy Queen. After we had eaten our burgers and were moving on to ice cream, he looked at me intently and asked, "Larry, are we going to do this? Are we going to form a partnership to impact the community by reaching the men in the marketplace? Are we going to do this?"

I knew he was serious. I answered, "Absolutely!" So right then and there we claimed Ezekiel 22:30 where it says, "I searched for a man among them who should build up the wall and stand in the gap before Me for the land that I should not destroy it, but I found no one." We offered ourselves to be that someone.

Before I met Skip, I had passion for men, but with Skip, I had a partner.

The first thing Skip did was invite me to join him in Kansas City to hear him speak to a group of men. He said, "meet me at Arrowhead Stadium." After arriving I was ushered into the players' locker room. I had no idea that the group of men would be the Kansas City Chiefs. I was amazed how Coach Skip connected with the players and coaches as he spoke of his football journey and his spiritual journey in such a clear, concise, and compelling manner.

That was the beginning of us traveling together and speaking to a wide variety of audiences. In the process Skip poured into my life and became one of a handful of men who have mentored me. He modeled and taught me "business bearing," how to engage with businessmen and how to present myself in a professional manner.

Back in Columbia we began a weekly meeting called Prime Time, for businessmen in the marketplace, that met from 6:30 to 7:30 every Wednesday morning. The goal of Prime Time was to expose men to authentic believers and the word of God in a gracious, relational, and authentic manner. Skip served as the emcee and then one of the leaders would share a brief insight from the Word on a relevant topic. This was followed by sitting at tables in groups of four, discussing the passage and their thoughts, observations, and possible action steps around the table.

Men loved the environment and atmosphere and they began to bring other men. A friend once said, "When you play a man's game, men come to play"—we found that to be true as we sought to see men become fully equipped and effectively engaged in knowing Christ and in making Him known. The name and some of the mechanics have changed but we are still meeting every Wednesday morning, and have been for over 30 years.

We also started other smaller discipleship groups for those who wanted to dig in deeper. Forums of Four, where four men met to study and pray together, and Men Sharpening Men, which were one-on-one get-togethers.

Toward the end of Skip's time in Missouri, we saw the need for a yearly citywide conference, where men could be encouraged and challenged.

At first it was a handful of guys and then pretty soon it was 20, then 30, 40, 50, and finally 100. Larry found that when the groups got larger than 75 men, it wasn't as effective. So he began to encourage and train other men to start their own groups. As of the writing of this book, Larry has more than 30 satellite groups of men running their own early morning discipleship groups in Columbia, mid-Missouri, and surrounding states. Hundreds and hundreds of men are meeting together to study the Word of God and grow as disciples and ambassadors of Jesus Christ.

Larry and I connected and became such good friends that I would take him with me when I went to speak in different places. He is an amazing storyteller, and we both spoke about what God put on our hearts. Jeff "Monty" would join us at times, and that made us a power team.

In the first year or two of being in Missouri, I had another mind-blowing opportunity. While I was a head coach in Boise, I met a man named Dennis Mansfield. Dennis has a powerful anointing on him to influence government leaders and make a real difference in the kingdom of God. We connected and found that we both had a vision to influence business leaders in the Boise area. We would get together as my schedule permitted to have coffee and encourage each other personally and in the ways that God was using us in the community.

While in Missouri, I heard about Bill McCartney, head football coach of my former alma mater, University of Colorado Boulder, starting a ministry in Colorado that encouraged men to be Godly leaders in their families and communities. The ministry was called Promise Keepers. Their very first rally was a small but powerful one in the summer of 1991. I had heard about it and was interested. Their second gathering was planned for June of 1992, and I really wanted to go. I read about their mission and got excited about the impact they could have. I called Dennis, whom I knew had the same vision to influence men for God.

Dennis tells the story of what happened like this:

The initial start of our relationship with the Halls came when Skip was head coach at Boise State University. My wife, Susie, and I had a few opportunities to meet Skip and Virginia. The four of us just hit it off. We loved them both right away and I asked Skip to be a board member of the Idaho Family Forum. We worked together while he was the head coach at Boise State but remained good friends when they moved to Missouri.

In 1992, Skip and I were talking on the phone. He had already moved to Missouri and was the defensive coordinator at Mizzou. On the phone he said, "Hey, are you going to go over to Colorado?"

I asked, "You mean for that men's group thing called Promise Keepers?" We talked about it and both thought it was a good idea. We gathered a group of 12 or 13 men to go there and experience what was happening. Promise Keepers had put on one gathering the year before for men in Colorado. That one had been attended by about 4,200 men. But this second one was expected to be a lot bigger. In fact, they were expecting 50,000 men.

Skip was not able to go because of his job, but he told me, "Make sure you talk to coach Bill McCartney. Tell him that I sent you." McCartney was the guy who had the brainchild of Promise Keepers. So the 12 of us drove to Boulder and the Promise Keepers conference. The first thing I thought as I entered the golden Buffalo stadium, was that it was a complete failure. We walked in expecting 50,000 men at the stadium but there were only 22,000. In reality it was a good-sized group, but it wasn't 50,000. Even though my first impression was that the place was half empty, the move of God on the hearts of the men there was unmistakable. There were business owners, corporate CEOs, construction workers, college students. God moved on everyone's heart.

There was so much joy. They ended that particular Promise Keepers with the song, "I Have Decided to Follow Jesus." It didn't feel to me like an ending but like a beginning. I always try to smell God's aftershave and go in that direction. And it seemed to me that Promise Keepers smelled like Old Spice. It felt good, it smelled just right. And so I came home and talked to Skip about the experience. We both got excited to share Promise Keepers with Idaho, knowing that the Christian men in the valley needed that kind of experience.

We knew where we needed to begin. We needed to contact the Promise Keepers' team and get them on board.

Skip and I reached out to them in July of 1992, soon after I returned from the conference in Colorado. We contacted them regularly from that summer through early December. We both reached out to Coach McCartney or his assistants who were running it before there were full-time employees. They kept telling us they wanted to keep it local and not plan meetings outside of Colorado. They felt like it should be a local ministry.

Well, finally in December we had them on the phone. And they were almost yelling at us, "Why are you asking us to do this?" And we said, "The Lord started this. He's the one saying it. I think he's been trying to tell you this for three or four or five months."

After we said that, there was a dead silence on the phone. They finally answered, "Maybe He is."

I think this answer spoke a lot about their willingness to follow the Lord.

They prayed about it and came back to us later that month. We could put on a Promise Keepers event in Boise, Idaho. We assured them we were not interested in duplicating their ministry. We wanted this gathering to be Promise Keepers. All we wanted to do was show them that it could be done across the country. They could touch so many men outside of Colorado.

Skip and I dove into organizing a Promise Keepers conference with the idea to develop a template. One that people could easily use to organize Promise Keepers' gatherings in other regions. We worked hard for four months, getting sponsors and advertising for the event. On May 1, 1993, we held the very first Promise Keepers outside of Boulder, Colorado. We held it in Boise at Hawks Stadium and Skip was the emcee. The stadium held 3,452 people and it was packed. Because I had worked previously for Focus on the Family, I was able to get John Eldridge to speak and Skip asked Jim Zorn. We had a great lineup of other speakers as well, including Chuck Snyder.

We had people from all over the Pacific Northwest attend. In a pre-internet world, it was extremely successful. The following year, Promise Keepers began reaching out to other states and holding gatherings around the country. They had seen that the model was reproduceable because of what we did in Boise, Idaho.

One of the sweetest things that came out of the event was a letter I received about 10 days later. It was from a wife, and she just thanked us for what we did. Her husband was a helicopter pilot and traveled all over the world. He didn't really have much free time but went to Promise Keepers and was blown away by the masculine Christianity of Jesus. He ended up accepting Christ as Savior. Four days after the event, he was killed in a helicopter crash. Her letter moved me to tears. I knew that if the entire event was for that one salvation, it was completely worth it.

God birthed a vision in us to influence men in Idaho, and that led to Promise Keepers leaving the safety of their local Colorado community to become a worldwide ministry.

Virginia Gets an Opportunity to Teach Once Again

About half a year after we arrived in Missouri, the Great Flood of 1993 happened. Missouri was a lot rainier than we were used to in Boise, Idaho, which is high desert. But having spent more than a decade in Seattle, we quickly adjusted and had no problem with the wet weather. That first summer of 1993 ended up being an exceptionally wet one. In July alone, we had six inches more rain than normal. We started hearing about places where the Missouri and Mississippi rivers were getting extremely high, not just in Missouri, but also North Dakota, South Dakota, Nebraska, Kansas, Minnesota, Iowa, Wisconsin, and Illinois. A lot of people were concerned, although most aspects of our lives were not affected. We made sure to take our umbrellas with us wherever we went, and outdoor events were moved inside, but when football practice started again, we all ignored the weather and did what we were supposed to do.

The communities outside of Columbia were a different matter, however. By August things in Missouri were bad. In fact, just down the river from us in St. Louis, the river reached 20 feet *above* flood level. In Missouri alone, flooding killed 25 residents and displaced the families from 55,000 homes. Booneville, a city about 25 miles from the University of Missouri's campus, was one of the hardest-hit communities. They lost whole neighborhoods to the waters when levees were either breached or destroyed completely.

After the waters started receding at the end of August, the larger community around Missouri had to face the cleanup and rebuilding process. More than just land and homes were destroyed; people were traumatized. This flood was bigger and more devastating than anything that had happened before.

Virginia got an opportunity to work with a team from the University of Missouri counseling kids affected by the disaster. She had gotten some training in counseling while we lived in Boise and found that she really enjoyed helping people. That fall, she heard from her friend, Linda Duffus, about a group from the counseling department that was putting together puppet shows for flood-affected children. She applied for an official position on the team and was accepted. For months she traveled around during the day to the various communities in Missouri and engaged the kids through puppet shows, entertaining them and helping them deal with the traumatic experience.

Virginia had another really great opportunity during this time. She was elected National President of American Football Coaches Wives Association. She oversaw and planned events to raise money for children's hospitals, the annual American Football Coaches Wives Association convention, and other events where coaches' wives got together and supported each other. I told folks that I live with a big shot!

A New Coach for the Tigers

About a year after being at Mizzou, the athletic administration at Missouri made a head coaching change. Due to a 3-8 season, they moved Bob Stull to an administrative position in the athletic department. Bob and I had coached together for 15 years. It was sad to see him leave as the head coach. They let go of all but two assistant coaches—myself and Curtis Jones, who had played at Mizzou. I had been the defensive coordinator and Dirk Koetter had been the offensive coordinator. Dirk moved on to Boston College for two years, then Oregon for two years. After that he took the head coaching job at Boise State.

University of Missouri coaches, 1993

University of Missouri coaches, 1996

The Mizzou administration asked me to stay and be the interim head coach while they looked for another head coach. I filled that role for several months in the offseason until they hired Larry Smith from USC. My role was basically to keep the team together and keep them motivated. I worked to keep them going strong in school and had some team meetings. I like to joke that I never lost a game as the head coach of Mizzou—but I never won any either.

Coach Larry Smith arrived and dove into transforming the football team. He focused on discipline and teamwork. We lost a few players who didn't like his style, but overall, it was a good fit. He

named me the associate head coach. I was the right-hand man to
Coach Smith, like I had been to Coach James. I did a lot of the
administrative responsibilities as well as coaching the linebackers.
He was a good coach, known for revamping struggling football programs, but his philosophy was different from anything I'd experienced before.

One of his major strengths was motivation. He would use
signs, object lessons, and demonstrations. In fact, Jeff Montgomery,
"Monty," was kept running: creating signs, buying rubber bands
(think "snap back" attitude), hiring a helicopter to drop tennis balls
on the football field (think "bounce back"), and organizing motivational events. One of my fellow assistant coaches made a sign for
Jeff's door that read "Monty's Sign Shop."

Jeff was such a great sport that we pulled a really good one on
him in our second year of coaching at Mizzou. He tells the story
really well:

*Amongst the defensive coaches, I was known for always being
upbeat. I was 26 and full of energy and confidence. I was always
smarting off and challenging the coaches to try and break me. I
worked late hours to impress them and tried to be positive and
keep a smile.*

*Early in the season, we went to Texas A&M. It was my first road
game under Larry Smith. I headed up to the press box where I
was going to be located with all of our notes, our game plan, and
our depth charts. I was on the headset with Skip and when he
called defensive plays, I wrote it all down on a chart. That was
my job.*

*We went down there in early September, and it was hot and
humid. They ended up beating the pants off of us 73-0. It was
our worst loss ever. We had to leave three players there because
of injuries—concussions and a serious leg injury.*

We got home the next day and Skip called me into his office. Being really serious, he handed me a letter with the Texas A&M letterhead on it. It was a letter supposedly from A&M head coach R.C. Slocum. It said, "Coach Skip, I just had to send this letter out because the game didn't go very well for you guys and I wanted to admit to you that one of our graduate assistants was walking through the press box and just happened to see one of your grad assistants leave. While he was gone, we got to see your depth charts, game plans, and other important information. I'm willing to admit to it after the fact."

Coach Skip asked what I had to say about it. I was so upset that I couldn't even speak. He told me that Coach Smith wanted to see me. I somehow got up the courage and walked out of his office. I got around the corner and was just about to walk into the head coach's office when Skip called to me, "Monty, come here real quick."

So I turned around and even though his office was only about 35 feet away, it felt like it took me an hour. Well, I finally walked into his office and all of the defensive staff was there and they were laughing their heads off. I was so confused.

A couple of them yelled, "We snapped ya. We finally broke you! You said you couldn't be broken!"

They had come up with this plan where the secretary had completely doctored up the letter. It wasn't from the head coach. The other team had not gotten to our important documents.

But that taught me humility in a funny way. And after such a serious beatdown, the staff found a way to bring some levity to our jobs.

We laughed about that one for months. Monty was such a good sport about it. Though we harassed him pretty regularly, he was a real encouragement to the coaching staff and to me personally. I saw him implement a lot of what I had been teaching and coaching into his own life and in those who he influenced. After the first year as a graduate assistant, he was offered the Assistant Director of Football Operations position for the next three years. I was very glad to keep working with him. His job didn't change much. He was mostly assigned operational and administrative tasks, but no matter what he was asked to do, he did it with joy.

Coach Charlie, one of the most influential mentors in my life, visiting at Mizzou

After three years of working with Coach Smith, I was nearing my 30th year of coaching. Virginia and I started talking about me retiring from coaching. As we reflected on the last three decades, we talked about how I had experienced an amazing career, working with legends, coaching up remarkable men, and being a part of incredible football programs. I had coached in the best stadiums in the country and coached with and against some of the best college coaches. It was bittersweet for me to think of not coaching football players anymore. I wasn't done working or coaching up, but I felt like my time in the football arena was done.

Because we were leaving Mizzou, Larry Glabe and others contacted the mayor of Columbia, Missouri. They asked the mayor to
name a day after us. Our friends and fellow coaches threw a going-
away party and the mayor proclaimed it the Skip and Virginia
Hall day.

I wasn't ready to retire in the traditional sense, but I would retire
from football. I was ready to re-tire: put on new tires and head in a
new direction.

◄ **12** ►

Recruiting for a Different Arena

Soon after making the decision to leave football coaching, I had a God-arranged meeting in the middle of an airport.

Rick Kimbrough tells the story:

As I was in the Salt Lake City airport and running from one terminal to another to catch my plane, I passed a few gates. At one of the gates, I saw a gentleman sitting by himself, minding his own business. He was reading a book, which was covering my view of his face. And he had this big ol' ring on from a bowl win. Well that got me very interested because I was a former college football player and still a huge football fan. I decided I had enough time to shoot over there and talk to him. I walked up to him and said, "Excuse me sir." The book came down and the gentleman greeted me. I continued, "If you don't mind me asking, what bowl game is that from?" He told me it was from the Orange Bowl and I asked him more about it. I ended up telling him I had played football at Ole Miss and we bonded immediately. He introduced himself and that's when I found out he used to be the head coach at Boise State. Well, that got me extremely interested because I was moving to Boise. My job with Aflac was transferring me there as the state director. We only spent about five minutes together but had a really good connection. I handed him my card and told him I would love to keep in touch and then headed for my gate.

A couple of days later, I received a call from Skip. He said he had been thinking about what we talked about. He told me he was at the end of his football coaching career and he would like to get together with me soon and talk about the coaching aspect of Aflac. He was interested in what we do and how we recruit and offer people a career.

I was interested in seeing where the connection with Rick and Aflac would take me, but I was also walking through every open door. One of those open doors was with an old friend. Over the years, I had stayed in touch with Jim Herk, my friend and fellow coach from Henning High School. Jim knew I was planning on retiring (or re-tiring) and called me to see if I was interested in joining his company. He was now the manager for a company selling heavy-duty construction equipment in the Phoenix area. The company was owned by another teammate of ours, Ron Offut. Jim asked, "Why don't you come with us. You can use your skills recruiting, team building, and that kind of stuff." So he talked to Ron, and they decided to hire me.

I was concerned about Monty's next steps. I knew his position at Mizzou was not a long-term one, especially as I was leaving. Lisa was also expecting their first child and Monty needed a stable income. I asked Ron and Jim about hiring him as well and shared all of the value he would bring to the company. Thankfully, they offered him a position as well. Monty and I flew to Phoenix to dive into work while our wives took care of the logistics of moving. While there, we also found housing. The wives arrived in Phoenix a few weeks later, and we all began life in Arizona in earnest. I began recruiting and team building for the company.

Unfortunately, even though I was enjoying the recruiting and team building, it was a really short tenure because Jim moved on six months after we arrived. When Jim left, I knew I wasn't going to stay; he was my main contact. And when I left, Monty would go as well.

Thankfully, I remembered Rick Kimbrough with Aflac. He was really happy to hear from me again. He told me, "You need to talk to Ron Sanders down there in Arizona. I'll connect with him and tell him about you." Ron was the state manager in Arizona for Aflac. We met and I told him about myself, my work with coaching and recruiting, and how I could see that benefitting the company. Through a series of meetings, we worked out the details. It was decided. I would make the move to Aflac. Ron and Rick took a chance on me.

Rick remembers it this way:

Ron and I started lining up places Skip could go. Skip met a lot of other state directors and started recruiting for Aflac at college job fairs, through sports academic departments, or directly with applicants. He also was able to do a lot of motivational speaking.

I had such a respect for Skip that when I moved from Idaho to Iowa, I would fly him in once or twice a month to recruit for me for two to three days. He did an awesome job and helped change the culture there.

I wanted my first recruit at Aflac to be Monty. I could see him fitting into the company really well. He was smart, a real people person, self-motivated, and dedicated. He would have been perfect. However, now that he and Lisa had a baby, they decided to move back to Missouri. They believed that raising their kids around family was important. I completely understood but was sad to see them go. The five years we worked together had been a joy for both of us.

I became the first true recruiting coordinator for Aflac. I started working in Arizona but soon expanded to working in a number of states. I went where they asked me to go. All my work pertained to recruiting, coaching, and building teams. I was excited because I fit so well with Aflac.

Ron Sanders shares about how we met and worked together:

I met Skip through Rick Kimbrough. I quickly found out that Skip has a magnetism about him. He is second to none about how he approaches people and makes them feel comfortable. I knew he would be a great recruiter for us at Aflac like he had been during his college football career. So I jumped at the chance to hire him.

From the very first year, I could see what an impact he was going to make. In fact, he ended up not just recruiting, but changing the philosophy of the management team. Skip's philosophy is that recruiting should not be an event. Recruiting should be a frame of mind. He taught the management team that wherever they are is where they recruit, whether that is in line at the grocery store, talking to their niece, or hanging out at the lake. You never know when you will meet the right type of person for our line of work.

He helped change the philosophy of everyone wanting to run ads or schedule a "recruiting event." He got them thinking about recruiting all the time—being on the lookout for the right kind of people.

By the time he left, he had recruited about half of my agency force—over 125 people. And over a third of my management team were people Skip had recruited. They developed and moved up in management later. He was excellent at finding the right kind of people with the right skill set. He was also amazing at connecting new agents with veteran agents who could mentor them.

He had an impact on so many people's lives. Personally, because of Skip and the success he helped me drive, I went from State Coordinator of Arizona and New Mexico to the Director of Sales for U.S. Operations in Aflac.

I felt like the leadership at Aflac pretty much just said, "What do you need?" They saw my gifts and skills and empowered me to do my job to the best of my ability. I started off contacting potential Aflac team members from resumes, but soon expanded to college campuses, looking for graduating seniors who would be a good fit in Aflac.

Due to my coaching background, I connected with college coaches and athletic directors. They usually had a good idea about who was looking for a job or a career focus after graduating and would be good in the role as an Aflac Independent Insurance Agent. I also went to career fairs to reach non-sports-focused students. I went to different colleges and universities and had two basic stops at each one: the Athletic Department and the Career Services Department. Those two departments were my fishing ponds at colleges and universities.

Recruiting All-American Sales Agents

The very first guy I recruited for Aflac was a football player from Arizona State, Glen Gable. I heard about him from the football coaches. He was a dynamic team player, very self-motivated, and had good people skills. He knew that after college he needed a career other than playing football and was interested in Aflac. Soon after graduation, he signed up to work as an insurance agent and dove in headfirst. I am happy to say he is still with Aflac, working as a District Manager in Arizona.

My second recruit was Kristi Goodell. I found her at the insurance class I took to get my license. She was getting her license too and didn't have a commitment to any particular company. I talked to her about Aflac and she decided to join the team. She too

has been with Aflac for over 20 years. I recruited Lori Murphy, a
crackerjack team builder, who became my District Manager, when
I became the Regional Manager. I also recruited a man named Bob
Jones, who became the top salesman in Arizona for Aflac. I had
first met Bob (or Bobby, as I like to call him) at the University of
Washington where his oldest son was attending school.

Bobby likes to share how our relationship developed:

*Skip Hall started attending a Friday morning men's Bible study
that I helped start. We became friends and our wives connected
at another Bible study, and so it was a natural thing for us to get
together often. We had dinner together about once a week the
entire time they were in Arizona.*

*I didn't work for Aflac at the time, but Skip would share about
his company and try and recruit me. I finally decided to look
into it and requested to follow the top Aflac salesmen around
for a week and see what I would be getting into. I did that and
decided I could and would do this. That first nine months of
working for Aflac was unbelievable. I made so many sales that
I made it into the top one percent of Aflac agents nationally. A
huge part of my success was because of Skip.*

*Skip was a great mentor to me. He was always telling me, "Bobby,
you can do this." Another piece of advice he always gave me was
the Five B's. His original Five B's were: "Be brief brother, be
brief," but he changed it for me: be brief Bobby, be brief.*

*He truly encouraged, mentored, and coached me. In fact, I have
an acronym for Skip. He was a true C.O.A.C.H.:*

Communicator
On top of his game
An encourager
Concern for others
Honesty and Integrity

C.O.A.C.H. really defines Skip. I met a lot of his players and they saw the same things too. He was there for them, not in their face, but reaching out and encouraging them. He really did coach 'em up.

One of my all-time best recruits was a young mom who was looking for a job to help pay for her son's therapy because he needed a bit of extra help. Her name is Gloria Guerra.

In October of 2002, I was a young mom at a job fair looking for a part-time job that could help my husband with our family expenses. I had two kids at home, one of which was special needs who needed therapy three to four times a week to teach him how to walk and talk and take care of himself.

I was walking around the big building where the job fair was taking place, looking at everything. I came upon Skip Hall's booth, which was a plain table with black and white documents. There was no color or game or anything to draw attention. It was right next to a booth for the FBI, so I walked by his table and was talking to the FBI recruiter about what kind of work they did. After asking me some questions, I soon realized I couldn't work for them because at the time, I was not a U.S. citizen. As soon as I started to walk away, Skip came out from behind his table and asked me if I was a mom.

He told me that working for Aflac was perfect for moms because it is flexible, and you can set your own hours. He told me that however much work I put into it, I would get that much return from it. He was a really respectable and engaging gentleman, and I was interested.

I met with him the following week at his office, which was an executive suite at a hotel. He explained the opportunity. He told me it was commission based, but it wasn't about selling, it was about educating people and telling them about an opportunity to invest in their health and future. There would be marketing, but I had a degree in marketing and knew what that entailed.

I was very interested after that, and I asked Skip what it would take for me to do this. He informed me that I would need to study and take an insurance license test. I found out it would be $500 and I realized I couldn't do it. I didn't have $500 and I would need childcare before that to have time to study.

Skip looked at me and made the most generous offer. He told me he would pay for my classes, my test, and my license. And on top of that, he would give me $500 per month for three months to put my two kids in childcare part time.

I asked him why he would do that for me, and he told me he believed in me. I thought about it and I was going to turn him down because I don't like owing anybody anything, but I had a God-moment and before I knew it, I had accepted. With that acceptance, I promised Skip and myself that I would do my very best and be successful.

He was so encouraging, convincing me that I could do it. He was very authentic.

Skip told me I would need to take three or four weeks to study for the exam and I told him I didn't have that long. I needed to take the exam as soon as possible so I could get working and make money. He believed in me so much that he bought me the books, and I studied for three days, Friday, Saturday, and Sunday, while my husband watched the kids. On Monday, I took the test and passed. Skip was shocked but really proud of me.

I worked hard for those first three months. I was knocking on doors, sharing about Aflac because nobody could understand me on the phone. My Spanish accent was very strong at that time. So I made connections with people and then called them for follow-up. I really owned the opportunity because I found that I really loved explaining insurance to people and figuring out how I could help them. It was work, but not hard. I was okay with rejection, and I would just move on. I only wanted to work with nice people.

In the beginning, most of my customers weren't Spanish-speaking. Skip taught me how to reach out to the blue-collar businesses. He was very strategic with who and where he taught me to reach out. He gave me really good advice and training to be successful. He verbally encouraged me and that was a trait I have passed on to my kids.

I worked so hard that after the first three months, I had made $13,000.

Aflac awarded the President's Club Award to the top 75 agents. After the first year, I was #7 out of the 75,000 Aflac agents. I was able to take my family on a trip given to the President's Club Award winners. We did that for seven years in a row.

I feel that God put me on the insurance career for my son. I not only learned about all sorts of insurance that could help him get the therapies he needed but it also provided us with the money we needed to pay our portion for those therapies, get a house that would accommodate him, and get a pool for his physical therapy. The insurance career God gave to me was an excellent career for me. Meeting Skip has been such a blessing and truly life-changing.

I recruited for Aflac all over the place through the Midwest and Southwest. I connected with two men who were Aflac Territory Directors, Mike Tomlinson and Lynn Barnson. They kept me busy, arranging for me to work in different cities in their territory. I couldn't even begin to tell you how many airmiles I used in a year. I would go alone and connect with Aflac's regional managers for the area I was in. I'd take him or her with me into the school's career services and athletic departments. We'd meet people and make connections so that when I left, the local Aflac managers were plugged in. Mike and Lynn believed in me and what I was doing.

Mike Tomlinson explains exactly how we recruited:

Skip would call and set up an appointment with the head coach. The Aflac Regional Sales Coordinator accompanied Skip to the meeting and outlined to the coach what we were looking for in terms of new Aflac team members. The head coach would usually connect them with athletic directors and career placement people. Skip did that at virtually all of the Division I schools in my six-state territory. He reached out to smaller schools as well. He had really good results.

Skip started doing that when I was the sales coordinator for North and South Dakota. When I became the Territory Vice President, I continued to bring Skip in to recruit and he also trained my sales managers. Toward the end of my Aflac career, I became the U.S. Director of Sales. Over the time I was in that position, I had Skip doing the same thing but this time his footprint was the whole United States.

At Aflac, we were looking mainly for character qualities in the same way I did with football players. We wanted salespeople, but they had to be people-people. They couldn't be the run-over-people-to-get-a-sale type of people. Aflac didn't want that. I wasn't just looking for sports players, I started looking at business majors, journalism majors, anybody who was good with people and had good character. I was looking for highly motivated graduates who wanted to do some good for people and build a great lifestyle for themselves and their families.

All of the people I recruited with Aflac brought tens of millions of dollars through sales that they made. I never made a sale, but I recruited the people who did. It was a good combination. I am very grateful for Aflac and all its wonderful people.

Recruiting for Aflac was very similar to recruiting for football, except that I didn't have video to consult. I talked to teachers and deans and academic advisors. I asked them a list of questions. Are they willing to come early and stay late? Are they hard workers? Do they have a good attitude? How is their integrity? They were different but along the same lines as the 10 hard questions that I had used for college football recruiting for 25 years.

In the spring of 2011, Aflac started co-sponsoring the Heisman Trophy. We had a core group of Aflac managers who went to games with clients, potential clients, brokers, and other important individuals. We called the core group the Aflac Heisman team. We were going to Alabama one year with Tom Giddens, the top guy at Aflac in sales and marketing.

Tom was a big Alabama fan. He called me excitedly and said, "Coach, we're going to University of Alabama next week. We're going to do our Heisman thing and do a pregame kind of deal. We want you and Virginia to join us."

I said, "Well, that's great because you know Nick Saban is one of my former players and a fellow coach." Tom was very excited to hear that and told me what a big fan he was. I responded, "You want to meet him?"

He answered in the affirmative, but then skeptically asked, "How we gonna do that?" I told him to give me a day and then I called Alabama and set it up.

On the day of the game, Tom, his wife, his two daughters, another couple, and Virginia and I went into the Alabama football facility. Boy were they in hog heaven. Nick came out and greeted us, signed autographs, books, and footballs, and took pictures. His staff gave us a tour of the Alabama football complex. Nick was very gracious that day even though it was game day. They were playing Tennessee and, as usual, won the game.

Coach Saban and Coach Petersen meet at the 2016 Chick-fil-A Peach Bowl

That was Nick Saban's first introduction to Aflac. When some of the head guys at Aflac found out, they decided they needed to talk to him and see if he would be interested in doing some Aflac commercials. Now Nick is one of Aflac's spokespeople on TV commercials. And he doesn't keep the money—he gives it to the University of Alabama. I think he looks nice in an Aflac blue jacket as well as Alabama crimson.

Friends Who Are Family

Our time in Arizona was not all Aflac. When we first arrived, we began attending Scottsdale Bible Church. We met the leaders and after a year or so, they asked if we were interested in facilitating an adult enrichment class. We jumped at the chance. We had started community connection groups wherever we lived and were eager to facilitate another and build relationships. We loved it and quickly connected with a few couples. Besides Bobby Jones and his wife, Jan, one other couple, Mike and Mitzi Reuter, became lifelong friends as well. We shared meals, prayer, and fellowship.

The Reuters became such close friends that we celebrated most birthdays and holidays with them, shared triumphs and challenges, and took vacations together over the years. Years later they talk about our friendship like this:

We met Skip and Virginia at Scottsdale Bible Church. They had been asked to facilitate a Sunday school class. Dr. Fred Chay was the teacher, and Skip was the moderator. He's a good emcee. He always opened the class and warmed everyone up with humor. Virginia was just everything, the encourager and the greeter and time keeper. She made everybody feel welcome.

Out of that, we formed the home fellowship group. We decided we would meet in the different homes of the couples who were involved. Skip facilitated that as well, encouraging and leading us, and yet he was just one of us.

It was while we were in a home fellowship with several other couples that we just clicked with Skip and Virginia. God really drew us together and we became like family. We had many movie nights, many game nights, and also many meals together. We celebrated birthdays together and even went on vacation together. We just became very close friends, and that has re-mained through the years. We traveled to Athens, Greece, and Turkey together, and the Mediterranean Sea, which was quite a fun experience.

One funny memory we have was when we were sitting in Athens at the base of the Acropolis having dinner. Skip was stuffing his pockets with rolls and said, "Listen Mitzi, you never know when we're gonna get another good meal." Since he and Mitzi did NOT like the Greek food and were such picky eaters. If they didn't know what it was, they were not eating it! So, he looked at her and said, "Mitzi, take some of those rolls and put them in your purse because you don't know what you'll get at the next meal!" We laughed so much on that trip.

We saw what Eugene Peterson calls in his book, "a long obedience in the same direction." That's what we saw in Skip and Virginia both. It was their encouragement and their walk with the Lord, as well as their marriage, their love for each other, that really strengthened Mitzi and me.

One thing Skip always used to say to us was, "We're in the trenches together." We went through some real hardships and turmoil in our lives, as did Skip and Virginia. And we shared such joy and great times, too. When I think about Skip and Virginia, there is nobody else I would rather be with in the trenches. They have been amazing friends to us and continue to be to this day.

We still visit Skip and Virginia regularly. Their house in Boise is by a small lake—a pond really. I'll never forget the time that we came to visit, and Skip wanted to go fishing. He got all this gear—waders, tubes that you float in, fishing pole, and net. He and I put all this garb on and we walked out their back door and out to the pond. It was hilarious. We got in the water, paddled out, and fished for a while. We never caught a fish, but our wives told us it was the funniest thing to see us two guys out there floating in these tubes. I think he used that gear one time and then never again.

Every time we visited, if we were there on the right Saturday morning, we joined them at their neighborhood brunch. These were just a bunch of people who lived in the same community— just a regular neighborhood of about 20 homes. Two Saturdays a month in the summer, they gathered, and the hosts provided breakfast and everything that went with it. We enjoyed meeting their neighbors and seeing how close they all were. These days people have fences, and they don't cross them.

Once when they were in Arizona on Skip's birthday, I saw him get text after text after text. They were all from men he had coached through the years, all reaching out to wish him a happy birthday. I marveled at that because these kids had dozens of coaches throughout their careers. He had truly coached them up and those kids appreciated him.

One of the things Skip says regularly is:

"People will forget what you said. People will forget what you did. But people will never forget how you made them feel."

And that's what he did. He made players and friends feel important and loved. That's just who he is.

We made many friends and connections during our time in Arizona. God brought friends and coworkers into our lives to encourage us and bless us. One of the people God brought in my life was the famous entertainer Glen Campbell. He became my golf partner and while driving around in our golf cart, he would entertain me with stories about other famous people such as Elvis. We always had a good time together.

While I was in Arizona with Aflac for eight years, I worked during the school year, and we spent the summers in Idaho, in Boise, where we rented a condo, and in McCall, where we had built a home on the golf course. It was convenient to fly back and forth to Phoenix for business or wherever else I was headed for recruiting and team building.

Chris had come back to Boise after coaching at North Texas and Morningside. Suzie still lived in Boise and had given us another granddaughter in 1999, Jadyn. Suzie became a single parent after her marriage ended, and she continued to be an amazing mom. A few years later, she remarried and gave us our first grandson, Tyler. We really enjoy being grandparents.

The last two years we were in Arizona, I was an Aflac Regional Manager. Finally, in 2006, the same position opened up in Boise, and we jumped at it. For a while, Virginia had wanted to move back to Boise to be closer to the kids and grandkids. She was ready to make it our full-time home again and this was our opportunity.

◄ 13 ►

Back in Boise

It was no sacrifice or hardship to move back to Boise. We loved the area and community and still had a lot of good friends we had kept in contact with over the 12 years we had been gone. And Suzie with Cassidy, Jadyn, and Tyler, as well as Chris were all there.

Immediately upon settling back in Boise, we reengaged with church, community groups, and friends. We were happy to see that one of the community groups we had started was still meeting together and we jumped back in as soon as we arrived.

Living in Boise gave me the opportunity to do something for my grandkids that I'd wanted to do for my kids but hadn't always been able to because of my schedule as a coach. Virginia and I made it a priority to attend our grandkids' games and school functions. We were the supportive grandparents cheering them on from the sidelines. It was amazing! Cassidy played volleyball and golf, Jadyn played volleyball and soccer, and Tyler played football, basketball, and baseball. Because of my coaching history, I had compassion for the coaches, seeing the plays and calls from their perspective and giving them the respect and support that I had gotten. Our grandkids were also great students of good character.

We were very deliberate about spending time with them and encouraging them. We spent summer and winter school breaks at our place in McCall, enjoying the snow in winter and the lake and golf course in summer. Those three grandkids are such a blessing to us and we are so proud of them. They all did well in school and were given academic scholarships to college.

One Mother's Day, Chris took us to a nice brunch in Boise. We were chatting and enjoying our food when out of the blue he told us, "I met somebody." Well, that was quite a shock for us. We almost dropped our forks. Chris had dated off and on and occasionally had a long-term girlfriend, but we thought he was a confirmed bachelor.

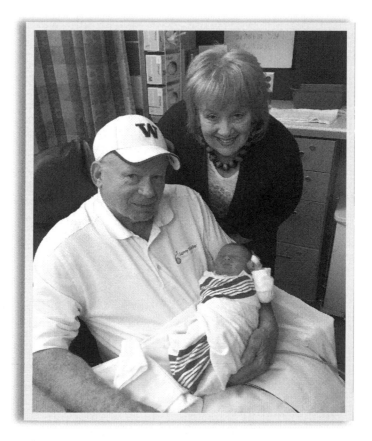

Our last grandchild, Austin, brings us joy and laughter

As he was telling us about her, we could tell right away that this was something special. Her name was Jennifer Yott and they had met on an online dating site. He told us they hadn't met each other face-to-face in the beginning. They just talked and talked prior to meeting in person. She and her family had moved to Idaho from California and lived in Eagle.

Soon after Chris told us about her, we got to meet her and liked her right away. She really seemed to fit with Chris. They got engaged shortly afterward and had a beautiful wedding. Two years later, they gave us another grandson, Austin. We were so happy for Chris and Jen.

Business Adventures With Chris

I worked with Aflac for two years full time in Boise and then Principal Financial Group came to me and offered me a job as Managing Director in Idaho. They said, "Here's what we need, and we think you're the guy. Here's what we're willing to do."

They had recruited Chris first and he became one of the top salespeople for Principal in the whole Northwest. Soon after Chris started with Principal, I joined the team. I couldn't refuse their offer.

I still did some recruiting for Aflac, but Principal was my main line of work as the Managing Director. I reached out to potential clients and brought them in to Chris, who is a genius with numbers and financial planning. We made a great team and I really enjoyed working with him. We were both doing what we loved and were good at; I not only recruited clients, but I also coached and did team building. Chris grew our clients' financial portfolios. We worked with Principal Financial Group for three years and then decided to go independent. In 2011, we started Hall & Associates Financial Services.

Owning our own business for the first time was both scary and exciting. But Chris and I dove in headfirst and worked to make the business successful for both our family and our clients. It has been a success. I am no longer working full time, but I still make some contacts and bring in clients. Chris is full-time Managing Director, handling the accounts and growing people's wealth.

Chris really enjoys the financial field.

I knew that if I wasn't coaching, I would want to be in finance. It is satisfying to coach people on their financial futures. I like numbers. I like watching charts and graphs and understanding them. I figured out that I really enjoy financial analysis and planning for companies and individuals.

Some people have a significant amount of money and that's their retirement. They can get really concerned when things are going crazy with the stock market or the economy. I found that I have to coach them well; remind them that we're looking long term. We're not looking for the flashy thing over there. We're coaching people on how the market works and how time and money work. We try not to let emotion get the best of them.

When we first started, we put our heads together and came up with a list of people who own businesses, and I set those initial meetings up to share with them what we offered and how we could help them. We got six or seven of the people from that original list as clients and that was our initial push. Since then it has been all referrals.

Hall & Associates does a lot of comprehensive things for small to medium size businesses; from retirement plans, exit strategies, and deferred compensation. We also do wealth management planning, retirement planning, and estate planning for individuals.

I worked under Don James for five years and his style still affects me. One of the funny things that makes a huge impact on me still is punctuality. To this day, I can't be late to a meeting. That came from him. Because if you were late to a meeting . . . let's just say, you couldn't be late to a meeting.

I know that seems small but there's tons of other stuff I learned from Coach James. He was so deliberate in his planning. He had goals and knew how to execute them. He was a master at finding people that could fulfill his vision. He was a really good man.

Roots in the Community

It seems like the older you get, the faster time passes. That has been true of my later years. Virginia and I grew deeper roots in God, our family, and our community over the years. God gave me the opportunity to connect with influencers in the Christian community, the sports community, and the business community. I began speaking more and more at sports functions, and business and church gatherings. I shared the lessons others had taught me and the lessons I had learned firsthand.

One of those lessons was from Coach Chris Petersen. He is an amazing man and was an incredible football coach. In his first year as head coach, he led the Boise State Broncos to an undefeated regular season. During the Fiesta Bowl that year against Big 12 champion Oklahoma, Boise State won 43-42 in overtime with a bold misdirection play for a two-point conversion. Because of that one game, Chris Petersen is considered a legend in Idaho.

What most people don't know is that six months later, during summer football training, he organized a campout for the players in the football stadium on the famous blue turf. They set up tents, played ping-pong and cards, and listened to loud music.

It was a party until Coach Pete dropped his Fiesta Bowl gear in a metal garbage can, poured lighter fluid on it, and lit it on fire. He asked his guys to volunteer their own gear to burn in the fire. Some did. He told his players that though there was a championship sign on the stadium, that was last year. This year they hadn't won a single game yet.

He told them to "Be. Here. Now." BHN. Don't look at what you've accomplished. Don't stay either wallowing in or glorifying the past. Be here now. BHN. That was one of Coach Pete's lessons on how to focus on the goal.

Hearing this lesson and many other lessons from both football and business coaches, I started thinking about hosting a radio show. I wanted to reach a wider audience and interview coaches, players, business leaders, and ministry leaders, sharing their stories and encouraging our listeners.

I had known Lee and Beth Schafer, who owned Inspirational Family Radio, which is 94.1 FM *The Voice* and 790 AM *Solid Talk* in Boise, Idaho. As a head coach, they had asked me to emcee their 25th anniversary radio event and I had thoroughly enjoyed it. It got me thinking about doing my own radio show. In 2017, after Virginia and I had moved back to Boise and I stopped traveling for Aflac, I reconnected with the Schafers and they asked me to do a daily radio show. I knew that was too much but I could see myself doing a weekly show. We talked about the vision and the purpose and *Game Plan for Life* was born.

Beth Schafer talks about our radio show.

Skip was the emcee for our 25th anniversary and did an amazing job. Even though his work had slowed down, he still had a lot to give and share. Game Plan for Life gave him the opportunity to impact the community that he loves. The years that he has been on the show, he has interviewed inspiring people, facilitating them sharing how God has impacted their lives and what they are doing now. Skip's encouraging attitude comes through, not only on the air, but also face-to-face. He is a living example of a Christ-like mentor.

Every Saturday morning at 10 MST on 94.1 *The Voice* and 790 AM *Solid Talk*, I interview coaches, players, and business and ministry leaders. I ask them for their stories. We talk about what God has done in their lives and we hear the lessons they have learned. It's been such a blessing to hear from people like Chris Petersen, Bryan Harsin, Chuck Swindoll, Kellen Moore, Cecil Andrus, Kristin Armstrong, and Andy Avalos. The radio show has given me a unique opportunity to help leaders inspire others the way I was inspired throughout my life.

Interviewing Suzie on *Game Plan for Life* radio show

One of the outstanding men I connected with after moving back to Boise was Jon Strain. Jon has a heart after God and we connected in our desire to influence and equip the Christian community in Idaho. As we met and got to know each other, we found ourselves challenging each other to step out and do things we had been reluctant to do. He was my Larry Glabe in Boise.

One day Jon was sharing with me about his financial need for the ministry that he was running, Search Boise. I knew just what to tell him. Jon recorded my story in his book *Spiritual Seeds*:

> *The tall Texas cowboy walked off the plane in front of Skip Hall, a 30-year college football coach. Skip had logged many travel miles, seeing many things over the years. Yet, arriving in Dallas, he found the cowboy first noteworthy, but, then, surprising. Noteworthy perhaps because the cowboy fit the stereotype: bowlegged, with the hat, the boots, the tight jeans (probably Wrangler), and a leather belt with a very large buckle. A true Texas cowboy, Skip thought to himself. They disembarked from the plane and entered the passenger boarding area. Skip observed the cowboy noticing something. Who wouldn't? It was a woman of uncommon beauty seated alone, apparently waiting for someone. Then came the surprise.*
>
> *The cowboy, no match for this eye-grabbing beauty, took the shortest path to her. He removed his hat, placed it over his heart and asked her, "Ma'aaam, are you awaitin' fer me?"*
>
> *Startled, she looked at the cowboy and matter-of-factly replied, "No. I'm not!"*
>
> *With balled fists, bristled arms and wincing facial muscles that cowboy disappointedly said, "D*MN!!" Placing the hat back on his head he walked away.*

After I finished the story, I looked at Jon and said, "You gotta ask." He was completely silent contemplating the story. I gave it a minute to sink in and then Jon started laughing out loud.

He told me, "I guess you're right. You gotta ask. If you don't, then the answer will always be no." He took the "you gotta ask" advice to heart and a couple years later started a ministry called You Gotta Ask. He wanted to equip Christians with the skill to engage in conversations with people searching for truth. He has found the best way to do this is to start with a question. In his book, *You Gotta Ask*, he calls this question the *Platinum Question.*

Because of my sports background, I have been able to connect with athletes and coaches who live or have retired in Idaho. One of those athletes I connected with was Bill Buckner. Bill was an amazingly talented baseball star who played for the Chicago Cubs, the Los Angeles Dodgers, and the Boston Red Sox. In 1986, he made a 10th-inning error in game six of the World Series that ended in a loss to the New York Mets. Both fans and the media publicly mocked him for years, blaming him for the "curse" that kept the Red Sox from winning the world series.

Bill handled it all graciously, but it took a toll on him and his family. He continued playing for a few more years, moving on to the California Angels, Kansas City Royals, and then back to the Red Sox. His baseball career spanned four decades and amazingly, he ended with 2,715 hits and 498 doubles. He batted over .300 average seven times with three seasons of 100 runs batted in. Despite his unbelievable talent, he still struggled with the one error at the World Series that seemed to define his entire career.

We started meeting and encouraging one another. He had gotten involved with real estate and a car dealership. Things took a bad turn for him (again) when he found out that his car dealership partner had forged his name on some illegal documents, causing Bill to owe a great deal of money. The partner then committed suicide.

Bill was struggling and I rallied some good Christian men to encourage him. We met weekly to pray, eventually adding in other men, and moving the focus to praying and encouraging each other. That group of guys still meets, over 12 years later.

In 2007, after the Rex Sox broke the "curse" and won the World Series, Bill was invited to throw the first pitch of the 2008 new season. He was reluctant to do it because of the years of written abuse that he had gotten from the media and fans. He came to us with his dilemma, and we encouraged him to do it. The world needed to see that they had not broken him. Thankfully, he heard us and accepted the invitation. It was an incredibly healing event for him. The packed crowd gave him a two-minute standing ovation. He came back home walking a little taller.

Another way I was able to reach sports and business professionals was by joining Price Associates. Price Associates is a team of like-minded business advisors and experts who help organizations and their leaders fulfill their visions by identifying and pursuing opportunities, solving problems, enhancing learning, and managing changes. I reached out to Ron Price, the owner and CEO, and we met for lunch. I told him I would like to join his group of leaders and speakers. Ron thought that was a good idea, but he wanted to check my references out.

Ron tells it like this:

When Skip first came to me about joining Price Associates, I told him, "Well first, I have to check you out more, Skip. I've heard good things about you but we don't bring anybody on our team without doing a thorough vetting of the individual." He gave me references so we could get others' impressions of who he was and what made him unique. I also asked him to complete one of our talent profiles so we could look at what his natural talent patterns were and what kind of skill development he had in regard to business leadership.

I asked one of my associates, Justin Foster, to do the vetting of Skip through the reference checks. One of the references Skip gave us was Chuck Pagano, who at the time was the head football coach of the Indianapolis Colts. When Justin connected with Chuck, they talked about Skip and what Chuck told Justin was that Skip had coached with him at Boise State. He told Justin that Skip was the best recruiter he had ever met. He'd never met anybody who could make somebody want to come play for you like Skip Hall.

I went back and talked to Skip about what Chuck said. Skip told me he connected with people by looking them in the eyes. "It's my two eyes and your two eyes. You build a relationship with people by demonstrating that you really do care about their success. That is the foundation for recruiting." He went on to tell me, "With student athletes, you make sure you include their mother in particular, because their mother has more influence on them than anyone else. And you make it personal, you make it about the individual."

As a consequence of that, I came back to Skip and said, "Okay, you passed the test." We invited him to be a part of the team.

Skip began speaking to businesses and leadership groups. One time he was invited to speak at a convention of the National Guard for the state of Idaho. I sat in the front row, videotaping. As he was speaking, there was an unusual response from the audience. There was sort of a sobriety or an engagement or leaning in that I hadn't seen with a lot of other audiences. I think they identified with his commitment to discipline and the correlations you can find between the military and a football team. Skip was really in the flow. He delivered his message with great heart and with great clarity. It was very succinct and at the end of that speech the whole place jumped to their feet to give him a standing ovation. That was the moment I was so grateful Skip was a part of our team. He gave them something that was not just in their head, but it had gone to their heart.

Skip has made a huge impact in Idaho. His goal when he came here as head coach was to revamp the football program. He wanted to set a high standard for excellence in football, academics, and character. Even though he left after a challenging football season, he felt that he had accomplished his goal. When he left, he left a piece of his heart in Boise.

When he returned almost 13 years later, he still had those connections, influence, and respect with the Boise community. He had this tremendous network of relationships anywhere from the former governor, Cecil Andrus, who he met with bi-weekly for a fellowship meeting with a bunch of other businessmen, to annual visits to the Boise State football program where he encourages the coaches. And no matter who the head coach is, they always welcome him in. He's done a tremendous amount of volunteer work in the valley. He's spoken to a lot of groups about what it means to be a leader.

His impact on the valley has been massive and he continues to radiate his character throughout Idaho. He continues to speak to and encourage young people all the way up to senior citizens. He is still following that same mantra. He wants to coach 'em up.

Another blessing in my later years was reengaging with Fellowship of Christian Athletes (FCA) in Boise. Some coaches from Idaho had been meeting consistently in a Coach's Huddle, but FCA in Idaho needed a strong leader who could impart vision and grow this impactful organization in Idaho. After looking around and evaluating those involved, they found Ken Lewis. Ken had been a biology teacher and wrestling coach. He had begun a Bible study with three athletes, but soon joined FCA and turned it into a Huddle. He had a passion for his students and a love for God. He had seen a need to encourage Christian athletes with other Christian athletes and had been taking Idaho kids to summer FCA programs in Oregon and Wyoming, but desperately wished to be able to offer the same experience to more students in Idaho. The board of directors approached Ken about taking over the FCA State Director of Idaho position.

He knew it was a massive responsibility, but after praying about it, he felt like it was the position for him. Ken immediately dove in headfirst, organizing FCA in middle schools, high schools, and colleges around the valley and planning an FCA summer camp. He soon saw the need in eastern Oregon as well and enveloped them into his area.

I help Ken in any way I can—I have emceed the Famous Idaho Potato Bowl FCA Breakfast and brought in inspiring coaches to share their heart like Tom Osborne. This breakfast is an opportunity to minister to the two teams playing in the Famous Potato Bowl in Boise, Idaho, as well as coaches and athletes in the Idaho and Eastern Oregon area. I had worked to create an FCA board while I was the head coach at Boise State. However, it wasn't until Ken Lewis took over as State Director that things really started to happen.

Ken shares about FCA in Idaho:

I first met Skip as a student athlete while attending Northwest Nazarene University. He was the head coach at Boise State. There were quite a few track and field students who started meeting together in an FCA huddle. Even though the track athletes had little to do with football, Coach Skip supported them and encouraged them.

Most coaches are only focused on what the players can bring to the game. Coach Hall was the kind of coach who cared about the heart behind the jersey. He was focused on improving skill and winning games, but not at the expense of the players' hearts and character.

Years later when I was the state director for FCA, I started getting to know Skip on a deeper level. I was so impressed that he truly cared about people. He went out of his way to encourage, build up, and connect people, including me and FCA. He was a great connector, calling me on the phone and asking how I was and offering to call this person or that person to speak or support FCA in Idaho. When he had challenging times, I was able to pray for him or Virginia. His heart for people truly reflects God's heart for people.

Another mentor and encourager I connected with after returning to Boise is my pastor, Bruce Young.

> *I met Skip originally as a casual acquaintance at various charity functions and community events until he started coming to our church, True Hope Church, Downtown Boise. Over the years Skip and Virginia have been in regular Bible studies, men's and women's ministry groups, and leadership boards. We have built a deep friendship and respect for one another, traveling together to ministry events or sports games. I have seen him in many situations, and he has proved to be a genuine caring mentor and coach.*

Many people think that Virginia and I led a charmed life. We did have amazing opportunities, working with revered coaches and players in top universities. However, there were struggles and difficulties along the way. We worked hard to overcome adversities, battles, and defeats. After 30 years of coaching and 20 years in the business world, little did I know that the hardest time of our lives was yet to come.

Carol James, "the Dawgmother," Virginia, and me at the UW Athletic
Hall of Fame induction of the '85 Orange Bowl championship team

◄ 14 ►

Living With Grace and Grit

Two things got Virginia and I through the toughest time of our lives: one was grace and the other was grit.

Grace is unmerited favor—it's getting what you don't deserve. It's unconditional love to the undeserving. C.S. Lewis once walked into a discussion about what made Christianity different than any other religion on earth. He responded, "Oh, that's easy. It's grace." C.S. Lewis was right. When the world likes to focus on karma, cause and effect, and earning rewards, God talks about receiving love, forgiveness, and provision through nothing we can do or strive for. The famous secular singer Bono put it best: "Grace defies reason and logic. Love interrupts . . . the consequences of your actions."

Virginia and I received that gift of grace in the beginning of our extremely hard situation. Then, in the middle of that struggle, we received the gift of grit.

The dictionary definition of grit is courage and resolve, strength of character. I have found that there are five characteristics of grit: courage, conscientiousness (carefulness and meticulousness), follow-through, resilience, and excellence (not perfection).

As a football coach, I needed to display these characteristics and teach them to my players. The football program made this possible. The way the schedule, critiquing, and practice were structured encouraged every one of these characteristics. Those players and coaches who didn't have grit didn't stay long in our football program.

However, even outside of sports, grit is a characteristic that is very needed. Grit is about overcoming opposition, doing your job and taking care of your responsibilities carefully and meticulously, following through, being resilient, and striving for excellence.

Our Life Changes

From the time Virginia and I moved back to Boise until 2017, our life together was filled with family, community, encouraging others, and enjoying each other. At my work, I shifted into a different role. I was not at the office as much, giving the day-to-day work to Chris. I spent time meeting and encouraging men, enjoying my grandchildren, sharing the lessons I had learned over the years with others, and getting together with other couples.

Virginia spent her days in much the same way. She loved being with our kids and grandkids, meeting and supporting women, and getting involved in the community however she could. She also regularly walked on the Greenbelt and was active and healthy.

Our 50th anniversary trip to Hawaii with the family

During that time, Virginia and I celebrated our 50th anniversary. Suzie and Chris surprised us with a trip to Hawaii. They arranged everything: housing, transportation, and meals. We all went to Hawaii and had the most amazing time. Being with our kids and grandkids on such a momentous occasion was a real blessing. Virginia and I both kept talking about how God had been so gracious to us in our family, our marriage, and our friends.

We had established deep friendships with people in Washington, Boise, Missouri, and Arizona. We visited some of them regularly. We would fly down about once a year to see the Reuters and others. I had made a habit of celebrating my birthday with them and with Dr. Walt Lippard, who shared my same birthdate, and his wife, Diane.

On January 24, 2018, Virginia and I were in our bedroom, packing for one of those trips to Arizona. Virginia mentioned that her right arm was hurting. The pain got so persistent that I decided to call our physical therapist to see if they had any idea what was wrong. As I was dialing the phone number, Virginia tried to tell me something. All that came out was a garbled couple of sentences.

I was shocked.

I immediately hung up the phone and called 911. As the operator was on the phone, I had Virginia sit down in her chair. We only had to wait a few minutes until I heard the sirens heading our way. The EMTs arrived, loaded Virginia carefully onto a stretcher and wheeled her into the ambulance. I followed closely behind in our car, praying silently the entire way to the hospital.

I called Chris while driving and told him what happened. He called Suzie for me. They couldn't quite believe it. Virginia had not had any physical or health issues lately. This came out of nowhere.

Once we arrived and the doctors saw her, they confirmed my biggest fear. My wife had had a massive stroke. The doctors called it a cerebral hemorrhage or a "bleed stroke." They are often fatal.

Suzie and Chris were there when the neurosurgeon was finally able to meet with us. He didn't have good news. He told us Virginia had suffered a massive stroke and that the bleeding wasn't yet under control. He gave us two unacceptable options and warned us that we needed to prepare ourselves for the worst.

Suzie remembers:

It was such a shock. My dad was the one who had a high-stress job and some physical issues but my mom was healthy. She walked every day and though she wasn't a big athlete, she always took good care of herself. When my brother called me and told me she had a stroke, I thought, where did that come from?

When I got to the hospital, I saw her acuity and everything decline. She started slumping. Since it was a bleed stroke, pressure was building up in her brain.

I'd never seen my dad lost like he was in the hospital room that night when the neurosurgeon basically said, "Go get your affairs in order. Do you have a living will for her?"

My dad had always seemed like the strong one, the get-it-done one. My mom's job had been to be the supportive one. But that night my dad seemed lost. He was silent. He didn't know what to do. He was at a loss because my mom's life was hanging in the balance. She had been the wind beneath his wings. I think we never knew how much he relied on her for emotional support.

So the neurosurgeon came in and said, "Well, either we let it swell and take our chances or we take off half her skull and let it relieve, but she probably won't have any quality of life." We all just looked at each other. We couldn't do either option. The neurosurgeon—we called him Dr. Death because he had no bedside manner—basically said, "Get her affairs in order," and, "See ya later."

As we discussed what to do as a family, we got some perspective; this single doctor was not God (though he acted like he was). We decided we needed a second opinion.

My dad reached out to his own neurosurgeon and asked if he would give us a second opinion. Dr. Little came in the next morning and brought another specialist, the best brain surgeon in Idaho, Dr. Duckworth. Dr. Duckworth evaluated her and said he could do a craniotomy. He could create a one-inch hole in her skull that would hopefully remove the pressure, yet not cause too much damage.

Dr. Duckworth saved my mom's life.

Once my dad had a plan, he was back in the groove. He was very adamant. "God's in control." He would say it over and over. "Modern medicine is great, but God is greater." That's what he clung to. We all did.

The doctor performed the craniotomy. We waited and prayed and waited and prayed some more. The doctors monitored her brain swelling and, to our relief, they gave us good news. The surgery had worked. The pressure had been relieved, and her swelling was starting to go down.

As the news spread, we had an outpouring of love, support, and prayer for Virginia and our whole family. Friends, fellow coaches, and former players emailed, wrote letters, and sent texts telling us how much they loved us and were praying for us. We were encouraged.

Our family rallied around Virginia. Suzie flew her adult daughters home. Chris and his wife were at the hospital every day. I felt like God was using this to knit our family even closer than before.

After Virginia was moved to a regular room, the physical therapists started working with her. At first, it was just for a short time each day. We anxiously waited to see any sign of improvement. Though she had a hard time talking, she started to be able to move her fingers and toes, arms and legs. She definitely struggled with her right side the most, but her eyes shone with determination.

The doctors were encouraged by what they saw. She seemed to have fully functioning mental faculties and tiny physical improvements daily. After being in the hospital for a few weeks, her neurosurgeon thought she would be a good candidate for Aspen Transitional Rehab and called the facility. After they accepted her, we realized that through God's grace, He was opening the exact doors that Virginia needed. Several weeks later, she was ready to begin full-time physical therapy and rehabilitation at St. Luke's Elks Rehab hospital. There she received more physical, speech, and occupational therapy.

So many people had reached out to love and support us that we decided we would set up an online website through CaringBridge.org. We arranged it so that Jadyn, who was at college at the time, would post daily updates. I would text her with updates and she would post them. People could send messages and read the updates on how Virginia was progressing through the site that was dedicated to situations like ours. The outpouring was so huge that Virginia got over 12,000 hits accessing the site for updates and to deliver messages. The website was a huge blessing for us because we could keep our friends and family informed about Virginia's progress.

It was during this time and afterward that we saw Virginia's grit shine through. She did not give up. Her attitude said *fight, try again,* and *overcome.* I was so proud of her. She responded to this massive life-or-death challenge. She pushed through, fought for progress, kept her attitude up, and slowly and painfully made steps toward recovery. She showed true grit.

Comeback Player of the Year

Virginia made so much progress that the American Heart and Stroke Association did a story and video on us and called her the Comeback Player of the Year at their annual luncheon.

Suzie was even asked to head up one of the American Heart Association's big events.

> *I was asked by the AHA to chair their annual Go Red for Women fundraiser. At first, I wasn't sure I wanted to do it, but when I learned that they also focus on stroke prevention, my mom became my reason. She agreed to being the survivor story for the event.*

The Hall women at the American Heart Association
Go Red for Women fundraiser

Because of the situation that Virginia was in, she became a player, and I her coach. I was there to support her to get a touchdown in any way possible. My focus was 100 percent on my wife. I still had responsibilities, but she took priority. The kids were there to support her too. They organized dinners, cleaning, and shopping, even though they were both running their own businesses and taking care of their own families.

Virginia became a big encouragement to the doctors, nurses, therapists, and caregivers who worked with her. Her joyfulness and positive attitude, even through the hard times, was a shining light to everyone around her. She put so much effort into her recovery that she had a huge impact on family and friends.

God gave me the gift of grit on behalf of Virginia as well. Our friends Mike and Mitzi Reuter tell it like this:

Skip Hall was steady during that hard time because Virginia didn't know what was going on in the beginning. He pursued every way to help her and then when she finally was able to talk and communicate, she would say, "I just can't do it." And he would say, "Yes, you can. There you go." He was coaching her up.

Not only did he coach his teams up, but he also coached EVERYBODY up. Including Virginia. "Yes, you can do it Virginia." It was beautiful.

My pastor, Bruce Young also remembers how my life changed.

The thing that most impressed me about Skip was his response to Virginia's stroke. I've known a lot of public figures and they all have a high social IQ and are very good around people. When this happened to Virginia, Skip was right by her side and took care of her. He is truly her number one caregiver, not leaving her for extended amounts of time and always being attentive and supportive. He stopped his life for her. I have been so impressed by him. He's a leader, speaker, and encourager with a lot of good friends, but I saw devotion, love, and commitment to his family out of the public eye. He stopped his public life and turned all his attention to his wife. It was really impressive.

Virginia was able to come home later that year. She had made so much progress that she could walk with a cane. She always had a good attitude, even when we had a hard time understanding her. She was consistently joyful, laughing and smiling through her therapy when others had to help her, especially when the kids and grandkids would come over.

Virginia and me with Baxter

Once Virginia was home, we were blessed with two encouraging supporters. We were able to find an amazing caregiver who has been such a remarkable assistant to Virginia. Jackie Ince shows up faithfully, works cheerfully, and has been a real blessing. The other supporter is our dog, Baxter. Baxter turned out to be a huge comforter and supporter, staying next to Virginia's side all day and sleeping next to her at night. I even took him to the hospital to visit her.

Our growth group of 14 members in Boise has also been a tremendous support. They have encouraged, supported us in prayer, provided food and fellowship, and ran errands. The women have scheduled lunches with Virginia regularly and our whole group meets once a week for a time of connection.

It has been a few years since that painful time, and even though she has not fully recovered, she continues to work hard at her rehab, be courageous, encourage others, enjoy her family, and trust God. I am so thankful that God brought her into my life as a 16-year-old kid.

Dancing with Virginia at our granddaughter's wedding

Virginia, three and one half years after her stroke,
lookin' good in the neighborhood

As I look back on my life, I can see that God had a plan. He was opening doors, bringing me coaches and mentors, gently leading me, and showing grace as I messed up. He truly coached me up.

Because of God, I have a story worth telling, lessons worth sharing, and love worth giving.

So much has happened in my life. I have been a part of great teams, witnessed great events, and known great people. Those things are important, but when I am gone, the main thing I hope people say about me is, "He was a man of God and he cared about others."

The Hall family, June 2021

Photo credit: Katelyn Kristine Photography

Conclusion

As I look back on my life, I am extremely thankful God had His hand on me. He has loved me from the very beginning. He gave me a mom who did the hard thing to protect and love her sons. He brought Coach Charlie into my life when I needed a mentor and father figure in my teen years. God gave me the most supportive and loving wife, who stuck with me through thick and thin. He also connected me with an incredible coach, Don James, who enabled coaching opportunities at amazing universities. God led me through open doors that challenged and blessed me. He created in me a passion to be the very best man, player, husband, father, grandfather, coach, leader, speaker, and friend that I could be. I am so thankful that God gave me the drive to pursue perfection, and along the way, I caught excellence.

My relationship with Christ, my family, and my friends are truly my legacy. I have had the opportunity to work alongside some of the best people on the planet. I pray that opportunities like these will come up for you as well. My hope is that you will be fearless and take them, knowing He will give you the strength to be successful as you work hard and lean into the power of mentorship: getting coached and being a coach, regardless of who you are and where He has placed you. It doesn't matter if you are a stay-at-home mom, a CEO of a corporation, a retired grandparent, a high school student, or a college football coach, He has brought and will bring people into your life for you to encourage, mentor, connect with, and coach up.

My prayer for you is that my life and lessons would awaken in you a desire to influence, encourage, and give others hope, model integrity, and live with excellence. God has put us on earth to build relationships, which are more important than accomplishments. You have a calling to be an example and lead others to become the best versions of themselves by encouraging them through your words and actions.

Coach 'em up.

Coach 'em up.

The main purpose of a leader is to keep hope alive.

Resources for Coaches and Business Leaders

Motivational Speeches and Team Themes

How to Use the Resources section:
This section was prepared for the leadership development of coaches at all levels and business leaders who understand the value of coaching. You may utilize and modify the themes and quotes for personal growth, development of pregame speeches, and to share as themes with your players, coaches, small groups, businesses, and other community leaders.

Some of these stories are in the main part of the book however these lessons are meant to be used or shared with your teams as stand-alone stories as you coach 'em up.

The Importance of Having a Blueprint

Plans lead to success. Without plans, it's easy to get lost, lose focus, and miss the goal. When coaching for colleges, I found that planning was one of the most important things coaches did. I was privileged to work under a man for 18 years who was a master planner. He planned every minute of every practice and planned the path to finding and recruiting the best high school senior football players in the country.

An article by Chris Landon of the *SB Nation* put it perfectly:

For James, the son of a blue-collar father, building the Huskies back up was a project that involved guts, grit and, most importantly, a blueprint. James did not aspire to install a quick fix and get rich off a few flashy seasons. To him, Washington wasn't some stopover on his career arc where his focus was to get some cheap wins and then move on. His focus was to build something that would endure and stand the test of time. To build something that the community would not only embrace, but would incorporate into their daily lives such that it would become part of their very identity. His blueprint was a process that consisted of the following components:

- ► **Start with the character of his players he inherited:** *take boys and develop them into accountable and mature men. Make them leaders and examples for future players to follow.*

- ► *Next,* **develop the identity of the team as a whole:** *the cornerstones would be toughness, fundamentals, defense, and attention to details.*

- ► *Third,* **develop a personal network:** *take your branded product combined with your emerging credibility and parlay that into a network of high school coaches and parents who would want to send their young men into your care.*

That was it, in a nutshell. No extreme offensive philosophies. No promises to players of NFL riches. No fancy uniforms. No snazzy shoe companies. Just an enduring identity shepherded by a credible leader and a decent human being. It was a great formula, but it took years to implement.

Coach James didn't walk onto the campus of the University of Washington and start winning games. He developed a program, a blueprint that brought in the best of the high school football stars and trained them to be excellent. He had a plan and stuck with it.

As good as Coach Don James was at planning, I eventually met a better planner.

Jeremiah 29:11 (NIV) says, "For I know the plans I have for you, declares the Lord, plans to prosper you and not to harm you, plans to give you a hope and a future."

I can now say without a doubt that God had a plan for me from the very beginning. Though I came from a fatherless family, at a time when most other kids had fathers, He had a plan for my life. God brought me "fathers" in the coaches who shaped my life and led me to Him. I learned to listen and wait for His plan for me and my family. I watched Him open and close doors and trusted his plan for my life, though it wasn't always easy.

All of the successes in my life have come down to planning. With the Lord's guidance, I have created plans and stuck with them. It takes discipline and trust. When the plan gets tough (and it will), the successful people stick with it and don't give up.

You must have your plan and stick with it. You must have a plan, develop it, put it into practice, and follow it through. Success is by design. Success doesn't just happen. Success is a result of the plan and system that you have and stick with day after day, year after year.

You must have a system. You must have a process. This is what Nick Saban is so good at. It's what Chris Petersen was so good at. Don James was so good at. We all had a system and a process.

The discipline of durability is the ability to stick with a plan, no matter the circumstance. Sometimes people will want to change this or that or the other thing, but the discipline of durability is sticking with the plan. If you do that, if you have a great plan and you stick with it, success will come. If you want success, do it every day; today, tomorrow, next day, next week, next month, next year. Do it every day.

Make a plan, follow the plan, stick to the plan.

No game plan, no victory.

"It's not the will to win that matters—everyone has that. It's the will to prepare to win that matters."

—Coach Bear Bryant

Mentorship—The Heart of Coaching

Mentorship is essential if you are trying to grow personally and professionally. Mentors are the people who give you advice, show you the truth, encourage you through open doors, or warn you when the open door is not wise. Having a mentor can mean the difference between succeeding or failing at life.

Being a sports player automatically gave me mentors. I learned the value of a mentor through my coaches early on in my life and when I had the choice to listen and learn, I chose it. I am thankful that my coaches were men of character and integrity, and they instilled those values into my life as well.

As a coach myself, I had mentors—other coaches who had coached longer than me, and I was a mentor to both players and new coaches. This role came naturally because I had such great examples of mentors in my own life.

Some of the greatest examples of mentors I have seen are Chuck and Barb Snyder. Chuck and Barb were the chaplains for the Husky football team for six years. During those years they both poured their hearts and lives into the coaches, the players, and anyone who had a need.

Barb shares about their time as chaplains:

As chaplains, we gave a chapel on Friday evenings where both Chuck and I would share about a certain subject. The meeting was only about 30-45 minutes. Most of the coaches and players attended even though it was not mandatory. In the beginning, there was very little response from the players. We found that with Don James in the room, the coaches and players took things really seriously. Finally, at one chapel, Don James laughed out loud at a story I shared. Well, that was all it took to break the seriousness. After that, we found that the players started to engage and respond to our teaching. They also started coming to us afterward to shake Chuck's hand and give me a hug.

We also met with the coaches, players, and their wives or girl-friends individually and just got to know them, pray for them, and love on them. Some of them were having personal problems and came to Chuck or me for advice, support, encouragement, and prayer. We both had many opportunities to share about the Lord with them and pray for both coaches and players. It was a wonderful time.

We found that half of our ministry was with the coaches. Chuck had a big heart for them and found ways to encourage them. He would pick up sweets and bring them to the late-night meetings the coaches held. We would also invite them to our home and have dinner with them and their families. We just wanted to love on them. It was a friendship ministry.

I had a lot of opportunity to minister to the coaches' wives. I would meet with them, especially when they were struggling. I was even able to pray with some and lead them to the Lord. That was how it was with the students too. I would meet with the players' wives and girlfriends, really anyone who needed me.

Not only did Chuck and Barb pour their lives out to the University of Washington football coaches and players, but they were also co-chaplains for the Seattle Mariners for 27 years. They were an amazing example of mentors for both men and women.

Though coaches are mentors automatically, to be a great leader, you need to choose to be mentored. You need to find someone who can speak into your life and challenge you. It is not always easy, but it is vital to growing personally and professionally.

I chose mentors in other areas of my life besides just coaching when I was an adult. I had two great spiritual mentors and two solid business mentors. I learned so much from all of these men and I owe who I am today to them.

"A coach is someone who tells you what you don't want to hear, who has you see what you don't want to see, so you can be who you have always known you could be."
–Coach Tom Landry

Teamwork Is More Than a Cliché

Teamwork makes the dream work. Though this sounds cliché, it is very true that everyone on a team must do their part in order to make the dream happen. This is not a new or novel concept. There are many clichés about teamwork:

"There is no I in team."

"Many hands make light work."

"A chain is only as strong as its weakest link."

"Teamwork is less me and more we."

No matter what we have heard about how necessary teamwork is, the truth is that working in teams toward a common goal is the only way to succeed.

The best example of this was in our third season at University of Washington. We'd had a hard first and second season, ending those two years at 11-11. The third season didn't begin any better. All of the coaches knew that the UW fans, boosters, and leaders were not going to stand for it much longer.

After our fourth game, Coach James called everybody into the team meeting room. We were one and three that season. Though we'd only lost by a field goal the last game we'd played, we had still lost. Don wanted every player, coach, manager, and trainer to rethink and rewrite their goals and determine how each person could help improve our football team, in an individual way.

We took it very seriously and wrote down things we could do to help improve it. We signed our answers and turned them in to him. Every person in the football program did it.

I wrote down specifics on technique drills to get the players better at what they did. I also determined to be more attentive to them about learning what we needed to learn. This would help to make sure they had a grasp on skills before they went out to the practice field, where they could practice it properly. With proper practice, they could apply it to the game when it really counted. I didn't want to assume anything.

That mental exercise was not only a season-changing moment that night in the team room—it was a program-changing moment. The next week at practice was like World War III in intensity. Players were flying around, attitude was great, and everyone was putting in 100 percent.

We went down that next Saturday and beat University of Oregon 54 to 0. During the rest of that season, we only added one more loss. We were the same team that started off 1-3 but went on to win the PAC-8 Championship as well as beat Michigan in the Rose Bowl.

The key to our success? Teamwork. Everybody upped their game. They took responsibility and determined what they could do to give 100 percent. Nobody was relying on anyone else to do their job or take their position. Everybody gave their all and when that happened, we won games.

"Championships are won by teams who love one another, who enjoy and respect one another and play for and support one another."
—Coach Tom Coughlin

Remember Your Why and Vision

Helen Keller was asked once, "Is it the worst thing in the world to be blind?" She replied, "No. The only thing worse than being blind is having sight but no vision." There is so much truth in this statement. You must have a vision. You must understand your why. Why are you doing what you're doing? What is the ultimate outcome you are working toward? What will be the result of all your hard work?

Vision is knowing what the end goal is. It is what keeps you motivated and working toward that goal.

When I was working on my post-graduate degree at the University of Colorado Boulder, in 1969, money was weighing heavy on my mind and the little I was bringing in didn't go very far. I started thinking about coaching at a good-sized high school, hoping that would be my next step to college coaching. In late spring of my first year, I heard about a large, well-known high school in Littleton, Colorado, that was looking for a head football coach. I couldn't pass it up, so I headed down there to interview. After a really good interview, they offered me the job. The school had such a great football program that the position included a house and everything. It was going to be a huge step up financially, which was a relief to both Virginia and me.

After I accepted the job, I got back to the University football office and Big Jim Mora Sr., one of the assistant coaches, was there. I said, "Hey Jim, I just got offered a job at Littleton High School."

He replied, "High school? I thought you wanted to be a college coach."

I hesitated then answered, "I do."

He asked, "Then what are you taking that job for?"

Well, that question hit me like a middle linebacker.

After I got home, I talked to Virginia about my dilemma. On the one hand, the high school job was at a very large high school with a great football program and good money. On the other hand, my vision was to coach college ball. Should I settle for what was before me or hold out for what I wanted? We decided to go for the ultimate goal.

I got distracted by the needs of the moment and took my eyes from the vision, the why. I will be forever grateful to Jim Mora Sr., who so simply reminded me of why I was doing what I was doing. I called the high school back, apologized, and withdrew.

As you work on the day to day, keeping the vision in mind keeps you from getting distracted and focused on why you are doing what you are doing.

"Live in your vision, not in your circumstance."
–Coach Chuck Pagano

Adversity Is an Asset

Most people work to avoid adversity. Adversity makes your life harder. It sometimes causes you to fail. It is certainly not fun.

Adversity comes in many forms. It is your parent telling you that you can't do it. It is a competitive company putting their prices lower than yours. It is struggling at school with the work. It is an opposing football team with a rock-solid defense.

But what many people don't realize is that adversity makes you stronger. When you try harder, you grow. When you struggle but don't give up, you get stronger—mentally, physically, emotionally.

We need to look at adversity as a positive thing. Can you gain muscle if you don't add resistance? Can you get stronger if you don't add more weights? In this same way, adversity is the weight that builds mental and emotional muscles.

As a leader, if we can set the example by facing adversity head-on, knowing it will only make us stronger, we can lead effectively.

Tom Landry said it best:

"How you handle adversity is more important than adversity itself."

I heard a story that illustrates this well.

Back in the 1800s, a sailing ship with a crew on board was sailing in open ocean.

One day the voice of the lookout from the crow's nest yells down, "Captain! Captain! There's a pirate ship off our bow!"

The captain hears and yells at one of the crew, "Bring me my red shirt."

A crewmate runs down, grabs his red shirt, and brings it up. The captain puts it on. The pirates come on board. There's a sword fight, but they repel the pirates and everybody's happy.

They sail on and in a couple days, again, the lookout's voice from the crow's nest yells, "Captain! Captain! There are three pirate ships coming at us off our bow."

Captain says, "Bring me my red shirt."

So the crewmate runs down, gets the red shirt and the captain puts it on. Sure enough, the pirates come aboard. There's another fierce sword fight but they finally repel the pirates and everybody's happy.

That night they have a banquet. They are so pleased. One of the crewmates stands up and asks, "Captain, how come every time we're attacked and under adversity, you call for your red shirt?"

The captain says, "I'm your captain. I'm your leader. I'm your example in the fight. If I get struck and start to bleed, I don't want you to lose heart."

And so they thought even more of the captain after that.

Then a couple days later once more from the crow's nest, "Captain! Captain! There are 10 pirate ships coming off our bow."

The captain yells out, "Bring me my brown pants!"

The humorous lesson here is that there will be days when it's clear sailing. Everything's fine. There will be days when the water gets a little rough and things get a little tough, and there will be days when it starts to get really rough. And then there will be the brown pants days.

I was asked in an interview once how long it took me to get over a loss as a coach. I responded with these words:

"I'm not sure that you ever get over a loss. I see losses in this light: they will help us become a better football team. Through a loss, we can learn some things about ourselves, about our team, that will help make us a better team the next week. I guess if there's value in losing, it's that it should help us find out what we can do to become a better team."

As leaders, we've got to work through hardship and be examples on how to handle adversity, knowing that struggle and resistance will only make us stronger if we can face it with the right mindset.

"If you can learn to use adversity right, it will buy you a ticket to a place you could not have gone any other way."
–Coach Tony Bennett, basketball coach at University of Virginia

The Price for Excellence Is Always Paid in Advance

Winning takes time. I'm not talking about the actual win itself. That can come in a single touchdown, a walk across the stage, a conversation with a boss. I'm talking about all the hard work that goes into the path that leads to the win.

Coach James is a perfect example of this. He had the best recruiting and practice schedule in college football. Yet he didn't start winning football games the moment he showed up at Kent State or the University of Washington. It took time. It took having a plan, hard work, focus, attention to details, learning through adversity, and showing up. Every. Single. Day. These were all the characteristics that lead to overall success. I have always encouraged other coaches to study the Coach James style of coaching. It became ingrained in me from the years we spent together. I highly recommend the book *The Thursday Speeches,* written by Peter Tormey. It has all of Coach James' speeches to the UW team about the upcoming game and about life in general.

Coach John Wooden was another example of extraordinary coaching. His success with UCLA basketball is renowned.

Although he had seemingly instant basketball success after he was hired at UCLA, in reality, he went through years of personal and professional hard work, self-discipline, adversity, and perseverance. From the very beginning, he was learning and overcoming challenges. He came from poor, humble origins where he could hardly afford to buy his entire basketball uniform, choosing instead to wear his jersey over his farm overalls. Despite this simple background, or perhaps because of it, the young John Wooden knew the value of a dollar and worked hard to put himself through college, sometimes digging sewers, waiting on tables, or selling sandwiches.

Everything he learned during those challenging times in his life led him to the unbelievable successes that came later in life. To this day, Coach John Wooden is known as "The Wizard of Westwood." Though he passed away in 2010, he is still regarded as one of the most successful college basketball coaches in the country. His coaching style, like Coach James', has been copied season after season, decade after decade.

Excellence is rarely achieved in a single moment. What sweat, tears, bruises, and pain did you go through to win that championship? How many years did you work for that diploma? What sacrifices did you make at work for that promotion? Excellence means sacrifices and consistent hard work. It's the goal at the end of a very long, hot, and rewarding road.

"Setting a goal is not the main thing. It is deciding how you will go about achieving it and staying with that plan."

–Coach Tom Landry

Understand the Times

It's important to understand the culture you live and work in, especially when times are tough. When facing challenges, it's important to evaluate circumstances and adapt.

An essential strength to have as a leader and coach is the ability to know what to do, which is knowledge, and when to do it, which is understanding or wisdom.

Because our lives and culture are always changing, everybody needs to have the mindset and ability to embrace change. We need to learn to be rigidly flexible. We all need to be able to stand up and hold fast to our values and convictions, but flex to the changes that inevitably happen around us.

When engineers design a skyscraper, they can't build it to be completely rigid. If they use materials that hold the building firm and inflexible, when a strong wind inevitably blows against the building, the structure would crack and break. For this reason, tall buildings are created with materials that have a certain amount of flex. Towers that are 1,000 feet tall sway two to three inches on a daily basis. In 50 mph winds, they sway about six inches from side to side, and in 100 mph gusts, these tall buildings can sway up to two feet without being damaged. In fact, the tallest tower in the world, the Burj Khalifa in Dubai, is 2,717 feet tall and slowly sways up to six feet at the top with no damage.

Engineers have the ability to create buildings that sway a lot more than six feet in regular weather conditions. However, they found that people couldn't handle the instability and would get sick. Because of this, buildings are built to be rigidly flexible. Skyscrapers can sway when confronted with storms without crumbling or being destroyed.

In the same way, we as leaders and coaches need to be able to sway when life brings us storms, or we will crumble and break. We also need to encourage and remind those around us that storms are inevitable. Experiencing them does not mean you are failing or even doing something wrong. Everyone encounters challenges. Staying rigidly flexible will keep us strong in times of change.

"Treat a person as he is, and he will remain as he is.
Treat a person as if he were where he could be and should be,
and he will become what he could be and should be."
—Coach Jimmy Johnson

Core Values Drive You

Core values drive your life. What's most important to you will lead you along the path you take. When your core values are about winning, wealth, or prestige, your choices will lead you down paths toward compromise, idolatry, and self-focus.

When we started winning at UW, I kept all my rings, watches, and medals in a little black box. I initially put them there to protect them. I pulled the box out occasionly and looked at each one of the accomplishments, remembering the triumph. When I committed my life to Christ in 1979, my core values took on an entirely new direction. As I gave more and more of my life to the Lord, I realized that those accomplishments had been my idols. My core value had been to win. I started to see that the black box couldn't hold what was most important to me anymore.

Four of my bowl game rings

When I spoke to various groups, I often dumped out my "trophies" as a way of showing them through an object lesson that living my life for Christ was much more important than any football or even leadership accomplishments. I knew I couldn't put God in that little black box. I didn't throw the box away; I was still proud of what we as a football program had accomplished, but I also acknowledged that even if I never won again, I would still follow the Lord no matter where He led. Matthew 6:33 says that if we make God's kingdom number one in our lives, He will take care of us and give us everything that we need.

In 1980, I had a chance to prove my core values.

I had an opportunity to apply for a head coaching position at a Division 1 university in Oregon. I had been coaching at Washington for a few years by that time but I was young—35 or 36 years old. After going through the process of applying and being evaluated, I became a finalist for the head coaching position at Oregon State. They let us know and wanted to schedule a visit for me to see the campus, meet the players, and meet with a panel of people from both the school and the community. I said, "That sounds good, on one condition. My wife comes with me, because we're a team." They agreed.

I was really excited about this possible job. It would have made me one of the youngest head coaches in college football at that time. I also knew I had a shoo-in because of my success at recruiting. I had recruited Oregon and stolen a lot of good players out of that state. They were probably thinking that if they could get me, they could keep the players in Oregon.

They got us down there for three days—Friday, Saturday, Sunday. While we were there, there was constant feedback from them such as, "You're the ones we want." Until the last day. On the last day, I met with a group of people. I was seated at the end of the table and people from all around the community and from the University were there, and they each asked me a question.

Things were going really well until we got to the 15th or so question. The man who asked it was an old rough fellow. He said to me, "Coach Hall, what's the most important thing in your life, and in five years where do you want to be?"

Well, I knew exactly what he wanted to hear and a year earlier, before becoming a believer, I probably would have said, "Football is the most important thing and in five years we're going to be in the Rose Bowl." They probably would have all gotten up and cheered and that would have done it. I would have gotten the job, hands down.

But that's not what I said. What I was led to say was this: "The most important thing in my life is my faith. And in five years I'll be wherever God wants me to be."

And that was the truth.

Well, you could have heard a pin drop. It was stone-cold silent and I could almost hear the wheels in these people's heads going around. "We've got a religious fanatic here!"

I didn't get the job.

I was told afterwards it was because of that answer.

That story illustrates the change that had happened in me because of my commitment to God. For the first time in my life, I knew who was Number One. God's Lordship in my life was the most important thing to me. It was my new core value. The Lord had saved me from myself and my own ego.

"Watch your thoughts, they become your beliefs. Watch your beliefs, they become your words. Watch your words, they become your actions. Watch your actions, they become your habits. Watch your habits, they become your character."
–Vince Lombardi

Motivation Is an Inside Job

Motivation comes in many forms—some positive and some negative, some temporary and some enduring, some internal and some external, some encouraging and some discouraging.

Lou Holtz started off coaching at William and Mary. One day they were playing Oklahoma, which was a bigger, stronger, meaner team, and it was a huge mismatch. On the day of the game, the news crew was setting up on the sidelines and the locker room doors for William and Mary burst open and the players sprinted out, running as fast as they could, diving for the sidelines. Then, Lou Holtz trotted out and the news people grabbed him and said, "Coach Holtz, what in the world did you tell those guys to get them so fired up?"

Coach Holtz replied, "Well, it was simple. I said, 'Men, today we're playing Oklahoma. They're big, they're mean, they're nasty. They want to knock your heads off. And the last 11 guys out of this locker room are going to start the game.'"

This is a humorous example of motivation by fear. Motivation by fear will last a short period of time. But what we're after as coaches is motivation of the heart. Coaches can help motivate you both on the outside and on the inside. The bottom line is the will to win comes from within. It's an inside job.

And that's the only kind of motivation that will last.

Inside motivation is like taking a shower. What happens if you don't take a shower every couple of days? You start to stink. In the same way, if you're not motivating yourself every couple of days or daily, pretty soon things will start stinking. You have to have a regular pattern or habit of motivation, like taking a shower.

"Talent determines what you can do. Motivation determines how much you are willing to do. Attitude determines how well you do it."
—Lou Holtz

The Five E's of Coaching

Coaching is more than somebody out there with a whistle and a loud voice telling you what to do. Coaching is about developing and valuing the heart behind the jersey using the five E's:

➤ Encourage – When you point out the good in a person, you inspire them to build on those characteristics. When you focus on what they are doing right, it motivates them on the inside to work and try harder.

➤ Educate – Giving the reason for the change, command, or rule helps others know and understand the whys of life. If they can understand the importance of what they're being taught, they will "buy in" and will motivate themselves.

➤ Edify – Educating someone morally or spiritually shows that you care about them as a person. You are not just teaching them their job, you are instructing their character.

➤ Exhort – Inside motivation takes emotions, the will to change. Exhorting happens when a coach or leader makes an appeal that reaches others' emotions.

➤ Example – Nothing you can say will make an impact if you don't do what you are telling others to do. The most powerful lesson you can give is with your actions.

The blend of these five E's is what you really want to do as you're building a team in the sports world or in the business world. You are working to motivate people on the inside and to do that, you need to appeal to their reason, emotions, and lead by example.

When you encourage, educate, edify, exhort, and lead by example, you are valuing people.

When I came to Boise State, Charlie was the video guy. He'd get up in the crane, the tower, or the cherry picker, and he would film every practice that the players and coaches would later look at for critiquing. He would do the same thing on game day. He was an invaluable part of the coaching and improvement process.

At the end of the first year that I was head coach, I called Charlie into my office and I said, "Charlie, I really appreciate the job you've done for us this year. You did a great job. I've got something here for you." I'd gotten him a nice blue sweater with the Boise State football logo and a white shirt to go with it. I handed it to him. As I stood smiling at him, his shocked face and open mouth told me nothing. I had expected a quick "thank you" and a handshake. Instead, I got big crocodile tears welling up and running down his face.

In alarm, I said, "Charlie, what's the matter? Is it the wrong size?"

He said, "No, Coach. I've been here 11 years, and nobody has ever told me I was doing a good job."

We need to value people. We need to reward people and tell people when they're doing a good job. That is a major part of coaching. It is such a simple thing to do, yet so profound.

"All coaching is taking a player where he can't take himself."
–Bill McCartney

Focus on the Goal

Chris Petersen is an amazing man and was an incredible coach. In his first year as head coach, he led the Boise State Broncos to an undefeated regular season. During the Fiesta Bowl that year against Big 12 champion Oklahoma, Boise State won 43-42 in overtime with a bold misdirection play for a two-point conversion. Because of that one game, Chris Petersen is considered a legend in Idaho.

What most people don't know is that six months later, during summer football training, he organized a campout for the players in the football stadium on the famous blue turf. They set up tents, played ping-pong, played cards, and listened to loud music.

It was a party until Coach Pete dropped his Fiesta Bowl gear in a metal garbage can, poured lighter fluid on it and lit it on fire. He asked his guys to volunteer their own gear to burn in the fire. Some did.

He told his players that though there was a championship sign on the stadium from last year, this year, they hadn't won a single game yet.

He told them to "Be. Here. Now." BHN. Don't look at what you've accomplished. Don't stay either wallowing in or glorifying the past. Be here now. BHN. That was one of Coach Pete's lessons on how to focus on the goal. He also had another acronym OKG, Our Kind of Guys, acknowledging a compatible culture that he wanted to foster.

For other coaches, it's other lessons. For Andy Avalos its LOF, Love of Family. For me it was "Together we win." TWW. And "What's important now." WIN. One of the years at Boise State, I gave my players a little round blue sticker to put on their watch faces. I told them that every time they looked at their watches and saw the dot, they were to remember, "What's important now."

Don James had quite a few good ones: NBR (nothing but roses); B2B (back to back); and others like that. We used these short motivational sayings to constantly remind ourselves and our players what to focus on.

We all need constant reminders about what to focus on. For football it's practice, teamwork, or winning. For business it could be clients, investments, or speaking. In our personal lives it could be family, health, or handling stress. Whatever it is, keeping the goal in mind and in view keeps us on the path to accomplishing that goal.

Be. Here. Now.

"I celebrate a victory when I start walking off the field. By the time I get to the locker room, I'm done."

–Coach Tom Osborne

Pursue Perfection, Catch Excellence

Coach Vince Lombardi's head coaching job with the Green Bay Packers began in 1959. He started with a now-famous speech. Bart Starr, who was a quarterback at the time, was there to hear it. He told it to me like this:

> When Vince Lombardi was hired by the Green Bay Packers, the first day the players and owners were to all assemble. Vince walked in and shook hands with the owners and said, "Thank you for this opportunity." Then he got in front of the players. To them he said, "Men, we're going to pursue perfection with a passion, knowing full well we'll never get there. But along the way we will catch excellence."
>
> When Vince got done speaking, Bart went and called his wife. He said, "Honey. We're going to win."

The players got behind the program and the things that Vince was sharing, and they went on to win five World Championships. The rest is history. But it all started off with, "How do you get to excellence? You pursue perfection. Along the way you catch excellence."

So the model became *be excellent.*

Be excellent needs to translate to all areas of your life—your core values, your personal ethics, your principles, and your behavior. There is no other way. When you pursue the very highest calling, every choice, decision, and plan becomes deliberate. You can't pursue perfection or catch excellence by accident—it must be a choice.

Choose to be the very best you can be.

> **"Perfection is not attainable, but if we chase**
> **perfection, we can catch excellence."**
> **–Vince Lombardi**

Don James Formula for Success

Coach James used this formula to lead his teams to National Championships.

Coaching Points:

Choose your team carefully

- ► Have people on the team who can't stand to lose.
- ► Big games are won by those who want to win the most.
- ► Ability is God's gift to man. Achievement is man's gift to God.
- ► Have people who are dying to succeed and dying to prepare to succeed.
- ► Find players who ask, "What can I do to help this team or organization?"
- ► Find people with good concentration to get consistency.

Evaluate everything

- ► Evaluation is important.
  - · Grade every player and every play.
- ► Have an objective system.
- ► Constantly strive to improve.
- ► Alter the objectives when needed.

Treat people fairly

- ► Treat people like family.
- ► Discipline is important. Use a regimented discipline program, not punishment.

➤ The #1 ingredient in a program is love.

· Find something to love in everyone.

➤ Don't spoil them.

· Everyone needs consistency.

➤ People will work as hard as they can if they believe their leader is competent and cares.

· They need to know that the leader won't collapse under pressure.

➤ Have an award system that recognizes everyone's contribution.

Team development

➤ Hustle. Give 100%.

➤ Show courage. The more courage we have, the more respect we will get, and the more productivity we will get from others.

➤ Know assignments. Mental mistakes will kill us.

➤ Care about winning. Must have a great desire to see the team win.

➤ Loyalty. Practice loyalty for the times things go bad. No finger pointing.

Motivation and goal setting:

➤ Write down goals

➤ Use John Wooden's Pyramid of Success

➤ Know the stats in order to create objective goals

➤ Motivated people:

· Are self-starters

· Never pass the buck

· Accept accountability

· Look for solutions

· Have tremendous drive and energy

· Hold themselves with dignity

Written Resources for Coaches, Teachers, and Leaders

Books:

➤ *3D Coach: Capturing the Heart Behind the Jersey* by Jeff Duke

➤ *A Coach's Influence: Beyond the Game* by Grant Teaff

➤ *Flock: Lead Your Tribe. Feed Your Team. Protect Your People* by Tom Roy

➤ *Game Plan for Life: Your Personal Playbook for Success* by Joe Gibbs

➤ *Heart of an Athlete: Daily Devotions for Peak Performance* by Fellowship of Christian Athletes

➤ *Quiet Strength: The Principles, Practices, and Priorities of a Winning Life* by Tony Dungy

➤ *Shepherd Coach: Unlocking the Destiny of You and Your Players* by Tom Roy

➤ *The Thursday Speeches: Lessons in Life, Leadership, and Football from Coach Don James* by Peter Tormey.

➤ *They Call Me Coach* by John Wooden

Websites:

- ➤ Athletes in Action - AthletesInAction.org
- ➤ Fellowship of Christian Athletes - FCAResources.com
- ➤ Run to Win - RunToWin.org
- ➤ Young Life - YoungLife.org

Podcasts:

- ➤ *Faith Out Front* – Fellowship of Christian Athletes
- ➤ *Game Plan for Life* – Skip Hall's Radio Broadcast as a Podcast
- ➤ *Heart of the Athlete* – Fellowship of Christian Athletes
- ➤ *Sports Spectrum Podcast*

Acknowledgments

This book represents a lifetime of love and support by my family: Virginia, Suzie, Chris & Jennifer, Cassidy & Vince, Jadyn & Gibson, Tyler, Austin, and the very tiny Selah. They have been my team through thick and thin.

The other team I have to acknowledge is much larger: my mentor coaches and business leaders Charlie Basch, Jake Christiansen, Rick Duval, Don James, Rick Kimbrough, Ron Sanders, Mike Tomlinson, Lynn Barnson, Tom Giddens, and Ron Price.

The other coaches I had in my life who were spiritual mentors include: Chuck and Barb Snyder, Chuck Swindoll, Jerry Mitchell, David Roper, Mark Traylor, Bruce Young, Harold Thomas, Jon Strain, and Joan Endicott.

My gratitude goes out to those who endorsed or did interviews for this book. If I missed any of you, I apologize in advance. Just know you are appreciated. Nick Saban, Chris Petersen, Linda Leoni, Jim Herk, Mike Rohrbach, Barb Snyder, Carol James, Mike Lude, Fred Goode, Chuck Pagano, Erik Helgeson, Bob Stull, Jeff "Monty" Montgomery, Travis McDonald, Larry Glabe, Dennis Mansfield, Rick Kimbrough, Ron Sanders, Bob Jones, Gloria Guerra, Mike Tomlinson, Mike and Mitzi Reuter, Chris Hall, Jon Strain, Ron

Price, Ken Lewis, Bruce Young, Suzie Hall, and Lori Murphy are among the group who shared great memories and stories that add to this book.

All of my fellow coaches had a huge impact on my life as well.

From Kent State: Dick Scesniak, Fred Gissendaner, Bob Stull, Sam Elliot, Ray Dorr, Maury Bibent, Ron Lynn, Greg Long, Dennis Fitzgerald, Jerry Hartman, George Greb, Don Lowe, Eddie Mullins, Dr. Tony Adamle, and Athletic Director Mike Lude.

From the University of Washington: Ray Dorr, Chick Harris, Bill Harris, Jim Heacock, Jim Mora Sr., John Pease, Gary Pinkel, Al Roberts, Dick Scesniak, Bob Stull, Chris Tormey, Trent Walters, Jeff Woodruff, Rick Huegli, Dick Baird, Allen Stover, Dennis Sealey, Dom Capers, Bob Wagner, Larry Slade, Denny Schuler, Mike Wilson, Dr. Steve Bramwell, Athletic Directors Joe Kearney and Mike Lude as well as the indomitable academic advisor Gertrude Peoples, my esteemed recruiting partners Abner Thomas and Laurel Lundberg, and the invaluable administrative secretary Cleo Blackstone.

From Boise State: Heath McInerney, Scott Pelluer, Jim Zorn, Pete Kwiatkowski, Chris Culig, Jeff Lindsey, John Gough, Dick Arbuckle, Jeff Murphy, Jay Mills, Herb Criner, Jeff Pitman, Chuck Pagano, Mike Snow, Carl Keever, Steve Burrato, Jim Fleming, Ron Thompson, Mike Lopez Jr., Jim Speck, Vince Alcalde, Gary Craner, Keith Brooks, Patti Morgan, Ron Debelius, Max Corbet, Dr. George Wade, and Athletic Director Gene Bleymeier.

And from the University of Missouri: Dirk Koetter, Bob Stull, Jeff (Monty) Montgomery, Larry Smith, Corby Smith, Curtis Jones, Moe Ankney, Jerry Berndt, Ricky Hunley, Andy Moeller, John Hoke, Steve Telander, Larry Hoefer, Dave Toub, Brian Stewart, Ken Flajole, Mo Latimore, Mike McHugh, Mike Ward, Harry Hiestand, Andy Hill, Rex Sharp, Bryan Maggard, Tom Scesniak, Garnet Payne, Bob Brendel, and Athletic Directors Dan Devine and Joe Castiglione.

The amazing Aflac team took a college football coach and gave him a chance to use his coaching, recruiting, and team-building skills in the business world: Rick Kimbrough, Mike Tomlinson, Ron Sanders, Lynn Barnson, Tom Giddens, John Thompson, Les Heinson, Greg Stenzel, Peter Sarantis, and others.

This book was financed by three great organizations: The Harold Thomas Foundation, my personal friend, Joe Russell, owner of Rocket Express Car Wash, and Cloverdale Church of God Boise, pastored by Tom Dougherty. Thank you so much for believing in my story.

The team at Aloha Publishing who made this book happen gets a huge thank you. To Maryanna Young, who has been encouraging me to write this book from almost the first time I met her over 20 years ago. Heather Goetter, who heard my story and my heart and wrote it down for all to read. Beth Berger, Megan Terry, and Jennifer Regner played various roles in editing, proofreading, designing, and bringing the physical book to life. I couldn't have done this without them.

The word "acknowledgment" can't convey the love and gratitude I feel toward everyone, mentioned and unmentioned, who had a hand in shaping, influencing, and encouraging me throughout my life. My heart overflows with love and thanksgiving for you!

About the Author

The threads that run through the life of Skip Hall are faith, family, and deep friendships. His loyalty in the coaching world is second to none, with many new stories shared in this book. For close to 30 years, Merle "Skip" Hall coached Division I college football, first at the University of Colorado and then at Kent State. Next, he served as the assistant head coach to legendary coach Don James at the University of Washington for 12 years, followed by a head coaching position at Boise State University from 1987-1992. He finished his coaching career as the associate head coach at the University of Missouri.

During Skip's football coaching career, he was a part of 12 bowl games—seven of which his team won, including three Rose Bowls. He had the privilege of coaching or mentoring Nick Saban, Gary Pinkel, Jim Mora Jr., Jim Zorn, Chuck Pagano, Jim Fleming, and Jay Mills—all highly successful head coaches in college or the NFL. Additionally, he coached dozens of players who went on to play in the NFL.

After his college coaching career, he became an extremely successful recruiter and regional manager for Aflac, continuing his passion to recruit, coach, and build teams—but this time in business.

He then began a financial services company, Hall & Associates, with his son, Chris. For the past 15 years he has consulted, coached, and been a keynote speaker for business management and leadership teams throughout the U.S.

Skip Hall is a superb storyteller, behind-the-scenes mentor, and dynamic groundbreaking leader with small group ministries, which still exist in four states. He started or grew divisions of Fellowship of Christian Athletes at the University of Colorado, University of Washington, Boise State, and Mizzou. He helped organize the first stadium-sized Promise Keepers event outside of Colorado. Skip is a longtime member of the American Football Coaches Association and an American Football Coaches Foundation Wall of Influence inductee. In 2017 he began *Game Plan for Life*, a weekly radio show to interview coaches, players, and business and ministry leaders. In 2019, Skip was named an Idaho Icon. He is currently a board member of the Idaho Youth Sports Commission.

Skip enjoys following college football, golf, and his grandchildren's sports and school activities. He and his wife, Virginia, who have been married over 55 years, have a tight-knit family who share special occasions, attend sporting events, and live the values of coaching 'em up.

If you liked this book, please give an Amazon review. It helps other readers and leaders find this book.

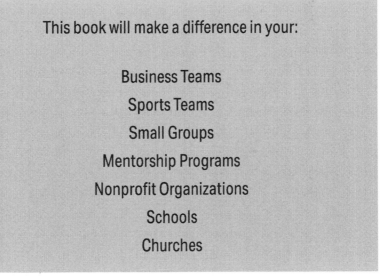

This book will make a difference in your:

Business Teams

Sports Teams

Small Groups

Mentorship Programs

Nonprofit Organizations

Schools

Churches

For quantity discounts contact Aloha Publishing
alohapublishing@gmail.com